STRANGE BUT TRUE
ALABAMA

Strange But True Alabama

ISBN: 1-58173-389-5

Design by Miles G. Parsons
Map of Alabama by Tim Rocks

Printed in The United States of America

Lynne L. Hall

SWEET
WATER

PRESS

Table of Contents

IN A STRANGE STATE: ROAD TRIP THROUGH STRANGE BUT TRUE ALABAMA 11

STRANGE STATUES 13

    Boll Weevil Monument.. 13
    Fire Ant Statue 14
    Hank Williams Sr. Statue 15
    Kaw-Liga 16
    Lady Liberty 17
    Metal Chicken Statue... 18
    Monument to the Hog.. 19
    Paul Bunyan Statue 19
    Peach Water Tower 19
    Peanut Statue 20
    Sand Mountain Muffler Man Statue 20
    Vulcan, God of the Forge 21
    Zirpa Anad Nitsurd Sculpture 23

NATURAL AND MANMADE WONDERS 25

    Ave Maria Grotto 25
    Cathedral Caverns 26
    DeSoto Caverns 28
    Dismals Canyon 29
    Natural Bridge Rock Formation 31
    Noccalula Falls 32
    Red Rock Corn Maze... 32
    Rickwood Caverns 33
    Sallie Howard Memorial Chapel 33
    Saturn 1B Rocket 34
    Shrine of the Most Blessed Sacrament 34
    W.C. Rice's Cross Garden 36
    World's Largest Office Chair 38

STRANGE MUSEUMS 39

    Alabama Cattlemen's Association MOOseum 39
    Anniston Museum of Natural History 39
    Arlington Antebellum Home and Gardens 40
    Berman Museum of World History 40
    Bessemer Hall of History.. 42
    Burritt on the Mountain 43
    Butch Anthony's Museum of Wonder 43
    Cook's Natural Science Museum 44
    The EarlyWorks Children's Museum.. 45

The Eichold-Heustis Medical Museum 46
The El Cazador Museum 46
The First White House of the Confederacy 47
Frog Museum 48
Historic Huntsville Depot 48
The Karl C. Harrison Museum of George Washington............................ 49
Weeden House Museum 49

THE HAUNTING OF ALABAMA 51
Confederate Graveyard 51
Drish Mansion 51
Fort Gaines.. 52
Huntingdon College's Two Student Ghosts 52
Pickens County Courthouse 54
The Plantation House 54
Shell Mound Park... 54
Sloss Furnace 55
Tinker Place 55
Tombstone of Nancy Dollar.. 56
University of Montevallo's Student Ghost 56
William Gibson's Grave 56

WEIRD HAPPENINGS 59
Big Foot 59
Hodges Meteorite 60
Jesus Door 61
Raining Catfish 61
Spaceship Landing 62
Stars Fell on Alabama 63
UFO Sighting... 63
The Virgin Mary.. 64

ALABAMA CREATURE FEATURE.. 65
Alabama Animal Hall of Fame 65
Bluegrass Farms Wildlife Sanctuary 66
Coon Dog Memorial Graveyard 66
Fred, the Town Dog's Grave 67
Harmony Park Safari 68
Leroy Brown... 68

EAT, DRINK, AND BE MERRY! 71
The Bright Star Restaurant.. 71
Ezell's Fish Camp 72
The Flora-Bama Lounge.. 73

Lambert's Cafe 75
Manci's Antique Club 75
The Original WhistleStop Cafe 75
Pink Pony Pub 76
Red's Little School House 76
Slick Lizard Smoke House 77

MISCELLANEOUS MISCELLANY 79
It's the Law! 79
Strange Town Names 81
    Bug Tussle 81
    Burnt Corn 82
    Eclectic 82
    Equality 83
    Intercourse 83
    Lickskillet 83
    Phil Campbell 84
    Possum Bend 84
    Remlap 84
    Scant City 85
    Scratch Ankle 85
    Slapout 85
    Smut Eye 86
    Three Notch 86
    Toadvine 86
    Trickem 87
Towns of Note 87
    Albertville 87
    Childersburg 88
    Fort Payne 88
    Gadsden 89
    Gee's Bend 89
    Huntsville 90
    Magnolia Springs 91
    Monroeville 91
    Montgomery 91
    Moundville 92
    Tuxedo Junction 93
    Wetumpka 94
World Record Holders 95
    Fastest Homebuilding 95
    Video Game Wizard 95
    World's Largest Cake 95
    World's Youngest Graduate 96

GROWING UP ALABAMA 97
  A Language All Our Own 97
  Folk Remedies 98
  Myths 100
  Old Wives' Tales.. 103

FUNNY HAPPENIN'S HERE 105
  Alabama Tale Tellin' Festival... 105
  Blessing of the Fleet.. 105
  Catfish Festival 107
  Chicken and Egg Festival.. 107
  Do Dah Day.. 107
  Dulcimer & Psaltery Festivals 108
  Dumplin' Days Festival 108
  Jubilees 109
  Mardi Gras 110
  Poke Salat Festival 111
  Rattlesnake Rodeo 111
  Soppin' Day Festival.. 112
  Strawberry Festival.. 112
  Trail of Tears Motorcycle Ride 113
  Watermelon Festival 113
  World Championship Domino Tournament 114
  World's Longest Yard Sale 115

PASTIMES PAST AND PRESENT 117
  Alabama Theatre 117
  Birmingham International Raceway 118
  Eternal Word Television Network 119
  Football in the Great State of Alabama 120
  Floating Condominiums... 126
  Gymno-Vita Park 127
  Rickwood Field.. 127

STRANGE BUT TRUE CULTURE 131
  Artists... 131
    Lonnie Holley 131
    Charlie Lucas.. 133
    Jimmie Lee Sudduth 134
    Mose Tolliver.. 135
  Inventors 136
    Mary Anderson 136
    George Washington Carver.. 137
    Bob Gallagher 138

Dr. James D. Hardy.. 139
Dr. Percy Julian 139
Waldo L. Semon 140
Music from the Heart.. 140
Alabama Jazz Hall of Fame 140
Five Blind Boys of Alabama.. 141
Sacred Harp Music 143
W. C. Handy 144
Writers 145
Truman Capote 145
Dennis Covington 148
William Bradford Huie 149
Kathryn Tucker Windham 151

SHOP 'TIL YOU DROP 153
Harrison Brothers Hardware 153
St. Nick's Knife Factory.. 154
Unclaimed Baggage Center 154

HISTORICAL EVENTS AROUND ALABAMA 157
Civil War Reenactments 157
The Battle for Brierfield Ironworks 157
The Battle of Decatur 158
The Battle of Fort Blakeley 160
The Battle of Mobile Bay 161
The Battle of Selma 162
LaGrange Military Academy 163
Tannehill Ironworks 164
Living History 165
Alabama Constitution Village 165
The American Village 166
Christmas at the Fort.. 167
The Fort Mims Massacre.. 167
Fort Toulouse/Fort Jackson 169
The Pioneer Museum 170
USS Alabama Battleship Memorial Park 171

FREE AT LAST 173
Montgomery.. 173
Selma 175

In A Strange State:

Road Trip Through Strange But True Alabama

Alabama is a state of contradictions. There's the Alabama that the tourism department calls "Alabama, The Beautiful." A tour of that Alabama takes you through breathtaking mountain vistas. Southward, you travel down magnolia-shaded lanes, past magnificent antebellum homes and verdant rural settings. Your tour concludes on the sandy tip-end of the state, where you can gaze out on the sparkling blue Gulf.

Beautiful.

Ah, but there's another Alabama lurking behind all that beauty, and it's a state of pure wackiness—a state filled with eccentric characters; extraordinary, weird, sometimes even spooky, places; and some of the most bizarre landmarks ever built. Join us on a tour of this strange but true Alabama!

Strange Statues

Alabamians love statues. Give us an event, an icon—heck, even a pest—and we'll erect a monument to it. Scattered willy-nilly across the state is an eclectic collection of eccentric monuments. We honor bumper crops and bumper crop killers, big men, big dogs, and big fruit. Next time you're tootling around the countryside, hit the back roads and check them out.

BOLL WEEVIL MONUMENT • ENTERPRISE

Not content to honor food, the folks of Enterprise have erected a monument to the boll weevil, that pesky little bug that chomped its way through the cotton crops of Alabama. It seems that what at first looked like a disaster turned out to be a blessing. Because of the devastation caused to the town's cotton crop, the good folks started growing peanuts and other crops. Diversity began and prosperity returned. The residents came up with the idea to honor the bug that renewed their financial vigor.

The Boll Weevil statue in Enterprise was originally erected in 1919. It is a monument to the bug that demolished cotton crops and ultimately brought prosperity to the region by forcing farmers to grow peanuts.

The original statue, built in Italy and installed in 1919, was a woman holding a spouting water fountain over her head. Thirty years later, some wag proposed adding a bug to the monument. A local artist fashioned a metal boll weevil and set it inside the fountain. It was promptly stolen. Upon its return, the weevil was affixed to the statue's raised hands.

Another act of vandalism brought international attention to Enterprise, now dubbed Weevil City. In 1998, two teenagers ripped the boll weevil from the statue's hands and buried it. The incident was reported by national and international media and was lampooned by cable network Comedy Central.

The culprits were quickly apprehended and the weevil disinterred. Unfortunately, damage to the statue made it impossible to return the weevil to its vaunted perch. The city did not remain weevil-less for long, however. A replica of the statue holding the weevil was soon erected and can still be viewed in downtown Enterprise.

It's no wonder that Alabama has so many statues, since the world's purest and whitest marble is reputed to come from Sylacauga. Alabama marble has been used in such prestigious buildings as the Lincoln Memorial in Washington, D.C. Samples can be seen in the Isabel Anderson Comer Museum & Art Center in Sylacauga.

FIRE ANT STATUE • NORTHPORT

Enterprise isn't the only city with a buggy statue. There's a giant red fire ant inside a tire (go figure) outside the Kentuck Museum in downtown Northport. It's a fitting tribute, since the stinging little pests supposedly entered the country via ships docking in Mobile Bay.

HANK WILLIAMS SR. STATUE • MONTGOMERY

Hank Williams' legendary career as a songwriter began here, in the state's capital. Born to a poor rural family, Williams was introduced to music by the hymns and southern gospel music in the humble log cabin where he grew up. By the age of seven, the poor health of his father forced him to sell peanuts on the street and shine shoes to help provide for his family. During that time, Hank learned to play guitar from a street musician named Teetot. A $3.50 guitar from his mother was his first instrument, and soon proved to be a good investment, since he immediately won first prize in a songwriting contest with his original composition of "WPA Blues." Although he never could

This statue of Hank Williams Sr. was dedicated on September 17, 1991.
Courtesy of the Hank Williams Museum

read or write music, he would author 125 songs before his untimely death on New Year's Day 1953. His voice was silenced then, but his legacy remains.

The city honored Williams' unparalleled career on what would have been his sixty-eighth birthday by dedicating a life-size statue (all six feet, two inches) of this famous country songwriter and singer in Lister Hill Park. It stands across from the City Auditorium, where Hank played many a concert and where his funeral (attended by 25,000 people) was held. He is buried just five minutes away in Oakwood Cemetery Annex. His final resting place is marked by a monument of Vermont granite that includes boots, a cowboy hat, and a poem by Audrey Williams.

Hank's statue is located in Lister Hill Plaza on North Perry Street. You may pay your respects at the cemetery on Upper Wetumpka Road.

KAW-LIGA • ALEXANDER CITY

You may know that the classic country song by this name, made famous by Charlie Pride, was written by Alabamian Hank Williams, but did you know it has another Alabama connection?

The song was penned in a small cabin on Lake Martin in Alexander City, where Hank had retreated in the summer of 1952, just months before his death. He and the Grand Ole Opry had parted ways, and Hank had called Bob McKinnon, an Alexander City disc jockey friend, to say he wanted to get away to McKinnon's cabin. It was already rented, so a local car dealer volunteered his instead.

The peace and quiet of the lake inspired Hank to write, and after learning the legend of the Kowaliga Indians, he wrote the popular song. (No one knows why he changed the spelling of Kowaliga to Kaw-Liga ... maybe to spell it more like it sounded.) The ballad in turn inspired the life-sized wooden Indian which today stands outside Sinclair's Kowaliga Restaurant on the banks of Lake Martin. Some say it was carved as a result of the song, but a more likely account says it was bought three months after Hank's death from a car dealership in nearby Sylacauga. Either way, it has come to symbolize the well-known song from the pen of one of country music's legends. Legend has it that the original wooden statue was so popular, visitors would come take a little wooden chip from it, and eventually wore the statue down to a nub. The replacement is there now, still reminding us of Hank's famous song, but this time, made of material as durable as the song itself.

The cabin where this popular tune, as well as "Your Cheatin' Heart," was written has been restored to its original décor and waterfront location on what is now part of Children's Harbor, a non-profit organization that provides camping and adventure services for seriously ill children and their families.

Kaw-Liga, the wooden Indian who "never got a kiss," and the cabin may be found just off Highway 63 on the southern outskirts of Alexander City.

> Hank Williams never lived to hear a recording of "Kaw-Liga," and he never saw the wooden Indian that his song inspired.

Lady Liberty • Birmingham

Give us your tired, your poor, your uninsured .... What better representation for Liberty National Life Insurance Company than a replica of the Statue of Liberty? At thirty-one feet and ten tons, Birmingham's Miss Liberty is one-fifth the size of the original and one of the largest replicas in the world.

Company president Frank Sanford Jr. commissioned the statue in 1951. Two American sculptors worked for four years to create the replica, which was then cast in France, much like the original. The statue was placed atop the Liberty National building in downtown Birmingham in 1958, where she reigned for thirty years.

In 1988 the company moved to new headquarters, and Miss Liberty moved, too. Today, she reigns from her new home in Liberty Park, just off Interstate 459 near Birmingham.

METAL CHICKEN STATUE • BRUNDIDGE

At first glance, you may think the metal chicken of Brundidge is just some yard artist's way of recycling. Actually, the 13-foot rooster, fashioned from chrome car bumpers, was created by a real artiste. Larry Godwin's work has been displayed in such far off places as New York City. He is, in fact, internationally famous, having crafted four exact replicas of the Wright Flier—the plane built by the Wright brothers— which sold for $200,000 each. And his work is featured in attractions throughout the state. (He's the genius behind Dothan's golden peanut.) In addition to the chicken, Godwin's Brundidge gallery is guarded by a gigantic metal

Alabama artist Larry Godwin fashioned the Brundidge metal chicken out of chrome car bumpers.
Courtesy of *The Auburn Plainsman* Stephen Atkisnon

sculpture of a creature with a fish head atop a set of muscular, slightly sexy frog legs, created by his younger brother Ronald. Very strange.

Located south of Brundidge on U.S. Highway 231.

MONUMENT TO THE HOG • DOTHAN

Speaking of metal animals ... Dothan has a big pig. The giant hog stands atop a large metal pedestal emblazoned Monument to the Hog. No information on its origins, but it stands outside a local feed store, which may have reason to pay homage to this notoriously hungry animal.

PAUL BUNYAN STATUE • STAPLETON

The logging industry is big here, which may explain the statue of Paul Bunyan located off State Highway 59 and U.S. Highway 31.

PEACH WATER TOWER • CLANTON

The Chilton County seat, Clanton is the state's largest producer of peaches, hence the water tower resembling a giant peach. The tower is 120 feet tall and holds 500,000 gallons of water. One of only two such towers in the country, it's a peachy sight, although some do

The Chilton County peach water tower is one of two such towers in the country.
Courtesy of Amber K. Henderson

say the bifurcation of the peach on one side makes it resemble a certain famous derriere!

The tower can be seen from Interstate 65 at the Clanton exit.

PEANUT STATUE • DOTHAN

From peaches to peanuts. Dothan is known as the Peanut Capital of the World. To emphasize this reputation, a giant golden peanut has been erected at the city's visitors' information center, and every year the city hosts the National Peanut Festival. The giant peanut is located at the visitors' center on Ross Clark Circle.

Dothan is known as the Peanut Capital of the World. A giant golden peanut statue stands in the Dothan visitors' center, a reference to the city's legacy.
Courtesy of The Image Agency

SAND MOUNTAIN MUFFLER MAN STATUE • ALBERTVILLE

Another big man is the statue of the Sand Mountain Muffler Man. He is located in front of the Camelot South Home Center in Albertville. For some reason, he sports a flashing blue light on one wrist.

Birmingham is called the Magic City because it was the fastest-growing city in the country in the 1900s. It grew like magic!

VULCAN, GOD OF THE FORGE • BIRMINGHAM

One of Alabama's most treasured monuments is the iron statue of Vulcan, the ancient Roman god of the forge. This 56-foot, 120,000-pound behemoth, the world's largest cast-iron statue, sports only a forger's apron, which leaves his exceedingly giant derriere—presumably the world's largest—exposed for all to see. This means that not only does he reign from his perch high atop Birmingham's Red Mountain, but he also moons the entire city!

So what is this big bare butt doing plopped smack dab in the middle of the Bible Belt? The idea to forge the statue came from a group of civic-minded residents of Birmingham who wanted an exhibit to enter in the 1904 World's Fair. The exhibit they envisioned would represent Birmingham's place as a major iron producer.

Vulcan, the ancient Roman god of the forge, stands atop Red Mountain in Birmingham, mooning the entire city with his exposed rear end.
Courtesy of Jay Taylor
www.BirminghmArt.org

Designed and built by famed Italian sculptor Giuseppe Moretti, the original statue held a spearhead in his outstretched right hand. His left hand gripped a hammer resting on an anvil. Vulcan proved to be a giant hit at the World's Fair in St. Louis, where he took first place in his category at the Palace of Mines and Metallurgy.

Strange Statues

Ah, but fame is fleeting! Upon his return to Birmingham, several women's groups objected to placing the statue in a proposed downtown park. He was ugly. And, goodness me! That bare butt!

So, instead, Vulcan was banished to the entrance of the Alabama State Fair, where the once-proud god became a shill for various companies. At one time, he held a jar of Heinz pickles; at another, a Coca-Cola. And, at one point, a pair of blue jeans was painted on, covering the famous bottom while hawking Liberty Overalls.

When, in the 1930s, the statue began falling apart (from humiliation, no doubt) and posing a hazard, the city considered melting him down for scrap. Luckily, the local Kiwanis Club intervened and raised money to repair the statue and place it atop its present spot on Red Mountain. A light was placed over the spear tip, which, for decades, informed Birmingham residents of traffic fatalities: green for no fatalities, red for a fatality.

Vulcan served as this colossal traffic beacon for more than sixty years, but by the 1990s, old age was taking its toll. Huge cracks had appeared, and the statue was in danger of crumbling onto the city below. A massive fund-raising effort was undertaken, and in 1999, Vulcan was disassembled and transported, piece by piece, across the state for a complete body reconstruction. (Yes, dear, there is a giant iron head on that truck!)

The $14 million reconstruction took five years, but Vulcan has been restored to his old glory. In early 2004, he was reassembled, to great fanfare, upon his refurbished tower on

Red Mountain. The traffic beacon is history. His outstretched hand now holds the original spear tip. And, once again, there is a full moon over Birmingham.

Vulcan Park is located on Red Mountain at Twentieth Street South and Valley Avenue.

Local legend has it that Vulcan, that sly dog, had a shocking romance with Miss Electra, the golden lady of Alabama Power. Miss Electra, a petite 23-foot, 4,000-pound, lightning-bolt-wielding bronze beauty, was placed (nude!) atop Alabama Power's corporate headquarters in Birmingham in 1926. Perhaps it was her coating of gold leaf that attracted him, but local newspapers reported a torrid romance between the city's two statues, complete with images of Miss Electra dressed as a flapper and Vulcan armored in rubber boots and gloves in order to safely buss his electrifying amore.

Miss Electra can be seen atop the Alabama Power Building in downtown Birmingham.

ZIRPA ANAD NITSURD SCULPTURE • FORT PAYNE

The aliens have landed on State Highway 89. Made of automotive parts and household appliances, this sculpture resembles a creature from another world. A sign at his feet introduces him as Zirpa Anad Nitsurd.

Natural And Manmade Wonders

Wackiness abounds on the byways of our alternate Alabama. No sappy theme parks here. Instead there's a weird hodgepodge of natural and manmade wonders. You can sit in the world's largest chair, learn the wages of sin and gain redemption in a garden of crosses, and relive bloody days in the weirdest of all bars.

AVE MARIA GROTTO • CULLMAN

Leading our list of wonders is Ave Maria Grotto, a world famous architectural wonder built on a miniature scale. Ave Maria Grotto is a four-acre park containing 125 diminutive reproductions of the most famous historic buildings and shrines of the world. Built between 1912 and 1958, the reproductions are the lifework of Benedictine monk Joseph Zoettl. They're constructed on the grounds of the St. Bernard Abbey, which, as Alabama's first and only Benedictine monastery, is itself a wonder.

The park's theme is heavily religious, populated by replicas of buildings of Jerusalem, scenes from the Holy Land, and various shrines to the Virgin Mary and other religious figures. Juxtaposed among the religious panoramas, however, are other historic tributes, buildings, and even flights of fancy. You'll find the Statue of Liberty next to buildings from Brother Joseph's native Bavaria. A tribute to the Red Cross workers of World War I adjoins the Temple of Fairies. Scattered around are the Parthenon, an American flag, the Leaning Tower of Pisa, the Alamo, and a pagan temple or two. Most items are set into spaces excavated from the hillside when the area was a rock quarry.

Brother Joseph began construction in 1912 as a hobby. In his construction, he used rocks, concrete, shells, tiles, and other materials available around the monastery. As his fame grew, people sent materials from around the world. He received bits of colored glass, chandelier prisms, seashells, jewelry, and glass floats from fishnets in Ireland, among other things.

Many visitors note that the scale on most of the buildings is off. There's a reason for that. Not being a world traveler, Brother Joseph had never seen many of the buildings in person. Instead, most were constructed from picture postcards, hence the one-sided perspective and skewed scale.

Brother Joseph died in 1961 and was buried at the Abbey. His work is well maintained by the Abbey and is open to the public. You can find the Ave Maria Grotto off Interstate 65, one mile east of Cullman.

CATHEDRAL CAVERNS • WOODVILLE

Outside this small town lies another of Alabama's natural wonders. Cathedral Caverns, once known as Bats' Cave, holds six world records:

1. The widest entrance of any commercial cave (25 feet tall and 128 feet wide),

2. The world's largest stalagmite (dubbed Goliath, this gigantic rock is 45 feet tall and measures 243 feet in circumference),
3. The world's largest "frozen" waterfall,
4. The world's largest stalagmite forest,
5. The world's largest flow stone wall, which measures 32 feet tall and 135 feet long, and
6. The weirdest stalagmite—35 feet tall and only three inches wide.

In addition to these sights, Cathedral Caverns, where the Disney movie *Tom and Huck* was filmed, has a crystal room. This room is not open to the public because the calcite formations here are so fragile that just the vibrations from a human voice could shatter more than 70 percent of them.

Located off U.S. Highways 72 and 431 between Woodville and Grant.

Cathedral Caverns in Woodville holds six world records.
Pictured here, the world's largest stalagmite, dubbed Goliath,
is 45 feet tall and measures 243 feet in circumference.
Courtesy of Nathan Wu

Natural And Manmade Wonders

DeSoto Caverns • Childersburg

Kymulga Cave, now known as DeSoto Caverns, is the first recorded cave in the country, and subsequently boasts the oldest cave graffiti in the U.S.

In the early 1700s, European trader I.W. Wright stopped for a respite in the cave and carved his name on one of the rocks. According to legend, the local Indians, who used the cave as a burial site, objected to this desecration and killed the hapless Wright. More than one hundred years later, a skeleton was found next to a rock with a name and a year inscribed on it. Can you guess? Yes, it was I.W. Wright, and the year was 1723.

During the Civil War, the caverns became a gunpowder mining center where the Confederate Army mined saltpeter, a vital element used in gunpowder. Fifty years later, Ms. Ida Mathis purchased the caverns to mine onyx, but the venture failed because the semi-precious stones could be mined more cheaply elsewhere.

DeSoto Caverns in Childersburg, first described in 1796,
is the first recorded cave in the country.
Courtesy of DeSoto Caverns

Prohibition brought about the cave's oddest and most notorious history. Local moonshiners, who used the cave to produce their intoxicating wares, opened a speakeasy inside the cave. Lawbreaking revelers from Birmingham and surrounding areas became regular patrons. Because of the numerous explosive fights, shootings, and stabbings, the bar became known as the Bloody Bucket. The bar was closed down when Prohibition ended in 1933.

After Prohibition, the Mathis family opened the cave as a show cave, displaying its natural wonders as a tourist attraction. Today, in addition to the beauty of the caves, visitors can see the rock where I.W. Wright signed his fate, as well as the sites of the Indian burial grounds, the Bloody Bucket, and where the Rebs mined saltpeter.

DeSoto Caverns Park is located southeast of Childersburg on State Highway 75.

DISMALS CANYON • PHIL CAMPBELL

There are several reasons the Dismals Canyon, one of the state's most beautiful sights, qualifies for our strange but true tour. First, and strangest, is the reason behind its name. It is named for the dismalite, a tiny glowing worm that lives in the moss on the canyon's rocks. At night, the green glow of these squirmy creatures casts an eerie light. They are so numerous that it's said to be difficult to know "where the dismalites stop and the stars begin."

The canyon is designated as a National Natural Landmark because of its geological and biological diversity. In this one area lies one of the oldest primeval forests east of the Mississippi River. There are two waterfalls, six natural bridges, and dozens of sandstone-sheltered grottos. Witches Cavern, located just below Rainbow Falls, is a labyrinth of moss- and fern-covered boulders. The cavern is given a supernatural glow from the large group of dismalites that reside here.

Dismals Canyon is one of the oldest primeval forests east of the Mississippi River and is rich in geological and biological diversity. Particularly famous are the glowing worms that live on the rocks that cast a strange green light at night.
© 2005 Ronnie Harris

More than 350 species of exotic plants have been identified in the canyon, with twenty-seven different species of trees growing within one hundred feet. Some of those trees shun the rich soils here and instead cling to boulders, wrapping their roots tenaciously around the rocky edges.

One of the most majestic sights here is the giant Canadian Hemlock, the largest of its kind in Alabama and thought to be the largest in the world. More than 350 years old, this behemoth stands 138 feet tall, measures 8 feet, 9 inches around, and has a crown spread of 50 feet.

Just as interesting, and strange, as the natural wonders of Dismals Canyon is its history as a hideout. According to local historians, Aaron Burr hid out here after killing Alexander Hamilton in a duel, and outlaw Jesse James eluded many a posse by slipping into the canyon.

Located on State Highway 8.

> The wild turkey is the official state game bird. It's also the unofficial state drink of choice!

NATURAL BRIDGE ROCK FORMATION
• NATURAL BRIDGE

This town is named after the curious rock formation located here. The natural bridge is just that, a rock formation that traverses a small gully. The longest natural bridge east of the Rockies, the sandstone and iron ore bridge is 60 feet high and 148 feet long. The park around it includes hiking trails, an Artesian well, picnic areas, accommodations, and a gift shop that features handcrafted items.

Located on U.S. Highway 278.

The town of Natural Bridge is named after this unusual rock formation, the longest natural land bridge east of the Rockies. Courtesy of J&D Richardson

Natural And Manmade Wonders

NOCCALULA FALLS • GADSDEN

Legend has it that Noccalula Falls is named for a breathtakingly beautiful Native American maiden whose bear of a father wanted her to forsake her true love and marry a man of his choosing. Rather than betray her love, the distraught maiden threw herself into the rushing waters over the falls and drowned. Grief-stricken, her father named the falls after her.

Located on State Highway 211.

Noccalula Falls in Gadsden is named after a Native American maiden who, in the face of an arranged marriage, flung herself into the water rather than forsake her true love.
Courtesy of J&D Richardson

RED ROCK CORN MAZE • TUSCUMBIA

The Red Rock Corn Maze is a ten-acre maze designed to test your trivia knowledge as you navigate the maze. Among the twists and turns, there are fifteen numbered pumpkin markers. Each pumpkin coincides with questions from a trivia sheet you select before entering the maze. Topics include sports, Alabama history, and general trivia. Right answers help send you in the right direction. Answer incorrectly, and you could be lost forever!

Located at the Walter McWilliams Farm, 2042 Red Rock Road.

RICKWOOD CAVERNS • WARRIOR

This underground "miracle mile" offers the secrets of the earth displayed before your eyes.

The Red Rock Corn Maze, a ten-acre maze in Tuscumbia, tests visitors' trivia knowledge.
Courtesy of Mike McWilliams
www.redrockcornmaze.com

Shell fragments and fossils of marine life are clearly visible along the cavern ceiling and walls. Formed by the force of water 260 million years ago, the caverns still contain active "living formations," as mineral-laden water droplets build colorful structures and flowstones. Guided tours take visitors past pools of blind cave fish, through numerous passages and beautifully lighted rooms, accented with thousands of sparkling white limestone formations.

The facility, which also offers areas for picnicking, swimming, and camping, is located off exit 284 on I-65 in Warrior.

SALLIE HOWARD MEMORIAL CHAPEL • MENTONE

Want some place truly unique to worship? Try the Sallie Howard Memorial Chapel. The church was built in 1937 by

Natural And Manmade Wonders

Colonel Milford Howard as a memorial to his wife. The stone church is built around a boulder, which serves as the pulpit. Services are held every Sunday. While you're there, you'll want to spend a little time appreciating the glory of some of those majestic mountain

The Sallie Howard Memorial Chapel in Mentone was built around a boulder, which serves as the pulpit. Services are held every Sunday.
Courtesy of Fort Payne/DeKalb County Tourist Association

vistas we mentioned. The church is located on top of Lookout Mountain.

Saturn 1B rocket • Ardmore

You may think your eyes are deceiving you as you drive along Interstate 65 into Huntsville, but they're not. That really is a rocket on the side of the highway. Perhaps Mr. Nitsurd misplaced his ride! Actually, the rocket is a 224-foot Saturn 1B rocket, which was used for experimental purposes by the Marshall Space Flight Center in Huntsville.

Located at the Alabama Welcome Center off Interstate 65.

Shrine of the Most Blessed Sacrament • Hanceville

Some entries in our list of strange places earn their spot because of their unique natures, but the Shrine of the Most

Blessed Sacrament is here because of the contrast of its beauty against an unlikely setting. In fact, some people describe it as being simply "in the middle of nowhere." But it's not surprising that there should be something different about it, considering how it came to be.

Mother Angelica, mentioned elsewhere in this book as the energetic and visionary founder of ETWN, was traveling in Bogotá, Columbia, several years ago. As she was going to pray one day, she saw a statue of a nine or ten-year-old Jesus in her peripheral vision. As she passed the statue, it came to life and said to her, "Build me a temple, and I will help those who help you." She didn't know what this meant because she had never heard of a Catholic church referred to as a "temple." But she later learned that the Temple of St. Peter was a Catholic Church and a place of worship, so her mission was clear.

Searching for land back in Alabama, Mother Angelica found more than 300 acres that belonged to a ninety-year-old woman and her children who were not Catholics, but when they heard what the property was needed for, the lady responded, "That's a good enough reason for me."

The resulting facility has been called "a wonder one could hardly expect to experience outside of Old World Europe, much less to find in the rural southeastern United States." The medieval-style monastery is home to the Poor Clare Nuns of Perpetual Adoration, a cloistered Franciscan Order. (Six "brothers" also live in the two-story white barn just inside monastery gates to help with manual labor.) The Shrine itself is located in the monastery's Upper Church.

Natural And Manmade Wonders

The interior of the chapel is exquisite, from its inlaid marble floors and high vaulted ceiling, to carvings in wood and stone. Stained glass windows from Munich, Germany, represent the nine Choirs of angels with individual windows depicting Archangels Michael, Gabriel, and Raphael, a Guardian Angel, and an Angel of the Apocalypse. The larger windows depict the Annunciation of the angel Gabriel to the Blessed Virgin Mary, the Visitation of the Blessed Virgin to Elizabeth, the Ascension, the Adoration of the Magi, and other scenes. The cloistered nuns of the monastery attend Mass here. An ordained priest hears confessional at appointed times daily in hand-carved confessionals. The Shrine is intended to be a "sacred place," set apart from the world outside. Photographs are not allowed, but most visitors agree that a photograph wouldn't do justice to the beauty found here anyway.

Respectful and conservative clothing is requested for visitors, but don't worry: If you don't have a thing to wear, appropriate apparel is available in the reception area.

The Shrine is located on County Road 548 in Hanceville.

W. C. RICE'S CROSS GARDEN • PRATTVILLE

Hell is Hot, Hot, Hot! screams one of the signs in the yard of a one-story brick home outside of Prattville. Hotter even than August in Alabama. Saving others from that eternal heat was Prattville resident W.C. Rice's mission in life, one he planned to fulfill through the construction of his cross garden.

Calling his garden Hell's Warning Label, he filled approximately eleven acres on both sides of the road with countless wooden crosses and crudely painted signs warning of impending doom and eternal damnation. One area of signs is labeled Sex Pit. Another area, strewn with empty beer cans, rails against drugs. Oh, yeah, and don't miss the sign offering to sell the entire garden for $5 million—CASH! (In a web posting on RoadsideAmerica.com, Rice raised that price to $25 million, ordered, he says, by God and Jesus to build a bigger and better cross garden.)

Rice began his garden in 1976, inspired, he said, by a wreath with a cross at his mother's funeral. Through the ensuing thirty years, commanded by God, he added cross after cross. And signs. Signs, signs, everywhere are signs.

You will die. Jesus saves. Jesus loves you. Repent. The world is coming to an end. Sex used wrong is the way to Hell. God said, "Read the Bible."

There are crosses and signs standing alone. Crosses and signs attached to the side of old shacks. Crosses and signs painted on the sides of abandoned kitchen appliances. There are even crosses and signs painted on Rice's old red truck. And, when he was alive, Rice himself sported crosses and signs.

Through the years, the cross garden and Rice received national attention, with numerous features in folk art books, magazines, and newspapers. Visitors from all over the country have signed his guest book.

Rice passed away on January 18, 2004, moving on, no doubt, to decorate a much grander garden. His earthly garden lives on, however, maintained by his family, on whom Rice expended many of his salvation efforts.

Natural And Manmade Wonders

You can find the cross garden just northwest of Prattville on Autauga County Road 86 off U.S. Highway 82.

WORLD'S LARGEST OFFICE CHAIR • ANNISTON

Should Vulcan ever go missing, the first place to look is Anniston, where the world's largest butt might be found plopped into the World's Largest Office Chair. At thirty-one feet tall and constructed of ten tons of steel, Anniston's big chair beats out all others (Yes, there are several others around the country!) for the title of the world's largest. The chair is located outside of Miller's Office Furniture, the company that built it.

Anniston is home to the world's largest office chair,
which stands at 31 feet tall.

Strange Museums

Alabamians have a strong sense of history, as evidenced by the large number of museums throughout the state. But you won't find works by Picasso or Monet hanging here. Nah. We're much more interesting than that.

ALABAMA CATTLEMEN'S ASSOCIATION MOOSEUM • MONTGOMERY

Beef: It's what's for dinner. It's also what's in the MOOseum: the Alabama Cattlemen's Association interactive museum devoted to the history of beef in Alabama. The MOOseum is staffed by Adam the animatronic, the MOOseum's official spokesman, who regales you with stories about his farm and his way of life and points you to not-to-be-missed exhibits. You can find out everything you never wanted to know about your favorite dinner. Little ones can tour Slim's Buckaroo Cattle Club, labeled The Children's Education Center, where kiddies learn of the nutritional value of beef and how many different things cow parts can be made into.

Kinda has us pulling for those cows on the billboards. You know, the ones that implore us to Eat More Chikin.

The MOOseum is located on the corner of Adams and Bainbridge Streets in the Alabama Cattlemen's Association building.

ANNISTON MUSEUM OF NATURAL HISTORY • ANNISTON

Explore the wonders of the world in seven fascinating exhibit halls at the Anniston Museum of Natural History. See one of the country's oldest exhibit of birds in their habitats, a vast array of wildlife exhibits, historical objects, and a killer Ancient Egypt gallery inhabited by two mummies.

Located in LaGarde Park, at the junction of Highways 431 and 21.

ARLINGTON ANTEBELLUM HOME AND GARDENS • BIRMINGHAM

Built between 1845 and 1850 by Judge William S. Mudd, one of the ten founders of Birmingham, the Arlington Antebellum Home and Gardens is older than the city itself. The Greek Revival building is the only antebellum mansion in Birmingham. It serves as a decorative museum that features a collection of nineteenth century furniture, textiles, and paintings. Historically, it was the site where Union troops planned the burning of the University of Alabama. It is a popular site for gatherings of all kinds, weddings in particular.

This beautiful reminder of a time past is located on Cotton Avenue.

BERMAN MUSEUM OF WORLD HISTORY • ANNISTON

Everybody's fascinated by a good spy story, especially one with a romantic link. Colonel Farley

The Berman Museum of World History in Anniston houses artifacts such as Hitler's tea service and Napoleon's dressing set. Pictured here is Colonel Farley Berman, an American spy who had a passion for history and souvenirs. Courtesy of the Berman Museum of World History

Berman, a native of Anniston, met his wife, Germaine, in North Africa during World War II. He was a member of U.S. Military Intelligence. She was a member of the French Intelligence. They were, in effect, spying on each other. But love transcends all. The two fell for each other, drawn together, perhaps, by a common love of collecting old things.

After the war, Berman brought his bride home to Anniston—along with a few souvenirs, which began his collecting binge. Over the next seventy years, the pair traveled the globe in search of interesting artifacts. He was hot for rare weapons. She preferred fine art. Their treasures—6,000 pieces, including hundreds

The Berman Museum of World History in Anniston houses historical artifacts collected by the spy couple Colonel Farley and Germaine Berman, who is pictured here.
Courtesy of the Berman Museum of World History

of bronzes, paintings, weaponry, and historical documents— are housed in the Berman Museum of World History in LaGarde Park, and it's definitely worth a look-see.

One of the most popular exhibits is the display of Adolf Hitler's tea service. There's also a rare Enigma decoder, used to break the German code in WWII, and an array of German uniforms and weapons.

The museum's Deadly Beauty gallery contains a rare collection of weapons and war memorabilia throughout history, including intricately decorated armor, Jefferson Davis's traveling pistols, Napoleon Bonaparte's ivory dressing set, and a set of spy weapons. The showpiece of the exhibit is the Royal Persian Court Scimitar, commissioned by Abbas the Great, Shah of Persia (now Iran) from 1588 to 1629. The sword's steel blade is surrounded with three pounds of gold. Its handle and scabbard are encrusted with 1,295 rose-cut diamonds and more than fifty carats of rubies. An eleven-carat emerald tops the hilt. Ya won't find this one at Wal-Mart!

The museum is located appropriately on Museum Drive in Anniston.

BESSEMER HALL OF HISTORY • BESSEMER

Hitler seems to hold a fascination for Alabamians. A few miles south of his tea set in Anniston, the Bessemer Hall of History contains the typewriter salvaged from Wolf's Lair, Hitler's headquarters near Rastenberg, East Prussia. Allegedly, Curator Mable Waites discovered

The Bessemer Hall of History houses Hitler's typewriter salvaged from Wolf's Lair.
Courtesy of the Bessemer Hall of History

this bit of history in the museum's basement in the mid-eighties. Unfortunately, she could find no ribbons to go with it, and Office Max is fresh out of circa 1940s supplies.

The Hall of History also contains Civil War memorabilia,

Indian and pioneer artifacts, and fossils. It's located at 1905 Alabama Avenue.

BURRITT ON THE MOUNTAIN • HUNTSVILLE

This unique museum of regional history is housed in the home of Dr. William Henry Burritt, homeopathic physician and inventor. The 167-acre site includes the Burritt Mansion, the Historic Park, and the natural mountain site.

The 14-room mansion, built in 1937, is shaped like an X (some say a cross), and is insulated with 2,200 bales of straw. The museum has changing exhibits relating to local culture and natural history. The historic park contains restored farm buildings with period furnishings dating to the 1800s. Authentically dressed interpreters demonstrate the daily life of 1850-1900 rural inhabitants of the area.

Of particular note are the miles of natural trails, including the award-winning Accessible Nature Trail, one of the first wheelchair accessible nature trails in the United States, and a model for others of its kind.

Perched atop Monte Sano Mountain in Huntsville, this Alabama site offers a breathtaking panoramic view of Huntsville and the Tennessee Valley.

BUTCH ANTHONY'S MUSEUM OF WONDER • SEALE

There be wonders here. More than 10,000 curiosities from around the world reside in folk artist Butch Anthony's Museum of Wonder. The collection includes the world's largest gallstone, a mummified cat, a human skeleton, and lots of other "art" collected by Anthony. One room contains hand-lettered signs with stuff like: Did you know that if you let a dog lick a sore on your foot, it will heal right up? Makes you wonder!

One of the greatest wonders may be the fact that Anthony has gained international fame as a folk artist. A former barbecue stand owner, Anthony began his incarnation by painting a face on a turnip. Surprised that someone bought that, he painted a picture. And sold it. Then he began collecting junk from the side of roads and using it to make art. He has traveled around the Southeast and even to a couple of foreign countries to sell his artwork. He also was chosen by our great state to create an ornament for the White House Christmas tree. He made a hand-turkey (you know, you made those in kindergarten) with George W. Bush's face drawn on the thumb.

The Museum of Wonder can be found outside of Seale on, umm, Poorhouse Road. Makes you wonder....

COOK'S NATURAL SCIENCE MUSEUM • DECATUR

Ewww! Bugs! At Cook's Natural Science Museum, you'll find plenty of them—roaches, beetles, termites, ants—all dead, thank goodness. The museum began in 1968 as a collection of employee training displays for Cook's Pest Control, one of

The Cook's Natural Science Museum was originally a collection of employee training displays for Cook's Pest Control. Today, the hundreds of wildlife exhibits are open to the public.
Courtesy of Cook's Natural Science Museum

The Cook's Natural Science Museum in Decatur is one of the few private museums that displays both bald and golden eagles. Courtesy of Cook's Natural Science Museum

Decatur's long-established businesses. The displays were so popular that the company's owner, John Cook Sr., decided to expand his collection and establish a museum.

Today, the museum inhabits 5,000 square feet and ranks as one of the most impressive natural science museums in the Southeast. Hundreds of exhibits include wildlife displays, colorful insects, birds, snakes, butterflies, rocks and minerals, and seashells and corals. It's one of the few private museums in the country authorized to exhibit endangered eagles. The museum displays both bald and golden eagles, an occurrence as rare as the birds themselves.

The museum is located at 412 Thirteenth Street SE in Decatur.

THE EARLYWORKS CHILDREN'S MUSEUM • HUNTSVILLE

The EarlyWorks Children's Museum takes the mystery out of history. Here at the South's largest hands-on history museum, kids can

The EarlyWorks Children's Museum is the South's largest hands-on history museum. Courtesy of the Huntsville Convention and Visitors Bureau

take a trip back into Alabama's early history. They hear stories from a talking tree, play tunes on giant musical instruments, build houses in an interactive architecture exhibit, and walk the gangplank of a 46-foot keelboat.

Take I-565 exit 19 and go South on Jefferson Street five blocks.

THE EICHOLD-HEUSTIS MEDICAL MUSEUM • MOBILE

Billed as the largest collection of medical memorabilia in the Southeast, The Eichold-Heustis Medical Museum in Mobile is a treasure trove of nineteenth-century medical exhibits. The innovative, the bizarre, and the downright horrifying reflect 200 years of modern medicine. The displays of barbaric-looking surgical instruments are guaranteed to give any child with tonsillitis the screaming meemies. Historical documents and photographs chronicle the day's practices of bloodletting and the bloody procedures of Civil War physicians. Also included are a quackery display and two larger-than-life papier-mâché models, one sporting a mustache and goatee.

The museum is located on the University of South Alabama-Springhill campus on Springhill Avenue.

THE EL CAZADOR MUSEUM • GRAND BAY

Want to see a real Spanish treasure? Visit the El Cazador Museum. The museum houses the remains of the *El Cazador*, a Spanish ship sunk in the Gulf of Mexico sometime around 1784.

Museum owner Jim Reahard researched the ship in Spain's Seville archives and learned that it sailed from Veracruz, Mexico on January 11, 1784. Bound for New Orleans, it carried silver and gold to boost the sagging Louisiana economy. For reasons unknown, the ship sank off the coast of Grand Bay and languished in its watery grave until 1993, when Reahard's nephew, fisherman Jerry Murphy, dredged it up by mistake— ironically on his vessel named *Mistake*.

At the museum you'll find gold and silver coins, jewelry, sword handles, the ship's anchor and bell, and other recovered artifacts.

Located at 10329 Freeland Avenue.

> The name Alabama is derived from an Indian tribe named Alibamas.

THE FIRST WHITE HOUSE OF THE CONFEDERACY • MONTGOMERY

On your tour of Alabama, don't forget to stop by the White House ... not that White House, The First White House of the Confederacy.

This two-story, white frame house was the residence of Jefferson Davis, his family, and his slaves while Montgomery was the Confederate capital. The Capitol was moved to Richmond, Virginia after the first year of the war because some thought accommodations might be better there.

The house later fell into such disrepair that some in the city began to lie to tourists about its actual location. The story goes that at least one cabby was so ashamed of the actual site, he would show tourists Morningview, the Houghton mansion, instead.

But help wasn't far away. The White House Association, which patterned itself after the Mount Vernon Ladies Association that preserved George Washington's home, was formed in 1900 and came to the rescue! Not only did the group bring the home back to its original glory, it transported it from the corner of Bibb and Lee to its current Washington Avenue location. After Mobile architect Nick Holmes Sr. had surveyed the house, dismantled it, and numbered every board, the pieces were moved and reassembled to its current location. It was dedicated at its new location on June 3, 1921. Visitors have included the comedian Charlie Chaplin and singer Donny Osmond, who was said to have asked for a copy of the plans so he could build a house just like it.

This famous structure is located on Washington Avenue in Montgomery.

THE FROG MUSEUM • BESSEMER

The Frog Museum is home to the World's Largest Frog, reportedly as big as a possum! The main entrance is manned, er, frogged, by the World's Rarest Frog. Put a quarter in the slot, and he'll serenade you with Frank Sinatra's "My Way."

Located on Cherry Street.

HISTORIC HUNTSVILLE DEPOT • HUNTSVILLE

Also located here is the Historic Huntsville Depot, one of the nation's oldest remaining railroad depots. Here you can climb aboard locomotives, see Alabama's largest public model railroad, and listen as Andy Barker, the robotic ticket agent,

tells about Alabama's railroad
history. There's also a Civil War
exhibit, with graffiti written by
Confederate soldiers, and a
children's corner with costumes,
train puzzles, and maps.

Located at 404 Madison
Street.

THE KARL C. HARRISON
MUSEUM OF GEORGE
WASHINGTON • COLUMBIANA

The Karl C. Harrison
Museum of George Washington
contains hundreds of items that
once belonged to George
Washington. You'll find family

The Historic Huntsville Depot, one of the
nation's oldest remaining railroad depots, has
a children's corner, a Civil War exhibit, and a
locomotive that you can board.
Courtesy of the Huntsville Convention and
Visitors Bureau

correspondence, jewelry, official correspondence and
documents, porcelain and silver table settings from Mount
Vernon, and many other prized possessions.

Located at 50 Lester Street.

WEEDEN HOUSE MUSEUM • HUNTSVILLE

Birthplace of Maria Howard Weeden, noted artist and poet,
this is the oldest house in Alabama open as a museum. Except
for the Civil War years when it was requisitioned for the use of
federal officers, this home was occupied by the Weeden family
until it was sold in 1956. It features Weeden's poetry and

paintings, which captured the essence of nineteenth century Southern culture. Especially interesting are her paintings of former slaves, which were used as the basis for slave costumes in *Gone With the Wind*.

Located on Gates Avenue in downtown Huntsville.

The Weeden House Museum is the birthplace of artist and poet
Maria Howard Weeden. The house captures the essence of
nineteenth-century southern culture.
Courtesy of the Weeden House Museum

The Haunting of Alabama

Mist rising on moonlit nights. Ghostly apparitions floating through hallowed halls. Strange and scary noises. Alabama can be a spooky place at night. With our past so rich in history, it's no wonder there are haunts wandering our land. Here's just a smattering of Alabama's legendary ghost tales.

CONFEDERATE GRAVEYARD • NOTASULGA

There is a Confederate graveyard on Union Camp Road that is said to be haunted by the spirits of Confederate soldiers. Late night ghostly figures and strange noises have been reported.

DRISH MANSION • TUSCALOOSA

Drish Mansion is an old plantation home in the middle of Tuscaloosa. Dr. John Drish built the mansion for his wife, Sarah. When Dr. Drish died, Sarah burned candles while he lay in state in the house. Reportedly, she became obsessed with those candles, locking them away and requesting that they be burned at her

The Drish Mansion in Tuscaloosa is reportedly haunted by the distraught ghost of Sarah Drish.
Courtesy of the Heritage Commission of Tuscaloosa

funeral. The family neglected her request. Shortly after her death, the tower where John had lain in state was reported ablaze. When the fire department arrived, the fire was gone, and there was no evidence of burned wood. This incident has occurred several times, and on one such occasion, the ghost of Sarah made an appearance.

FORT GAINES • DAUPHIN ISLAND

Fort Gaines is reportedly haunted by soldiers who died there.

HUNTINGDON COLLEGE'S TWO STUDENT GHOSTS • MONTGOMERY

Fort Gaines at Dauphin Island is reportedly haunted by dead soldiers.
Courtesy of J&D Richardson

Huntingdon College has two student ghosts: the Red Lady and the Ghost on the Green. Legend has it that both are the spirits of students who committed suicide on the campus. The Red Lady is supposedly a girl who was lonely and unpopular. Her fellow students taunted her because of her shyness and the fact that she wore only red. Distraught, she hung herself in her dorm room. Today, students have reported late night encounters with a young woman dressed in red who vanishes through doors and walls. There are also reports of a chilly blast of air whenever there's harassment by malicious students.

The Ghost on the Green allegedly killed himself after being jilted by a girlfriend who accused him of being too clingy. Unable to cope with the rejection, the young man shot himself on the campus green in the dead of night. While there have been no sightings, every year there are reports of students feeling someone tugging on their clothes or blowing in their ears when walking across the campus green at night.

Annie Ford died of pneumonia on March 26, 1891, and was buried in LaGrange Cemetery near Muscle Shoals. When her husband returned home from a trip to Chattanooga, he found that she had been buried in the wrong spot. It took more than a year to get the state's permission to disinter the body and move it to the right spot, but finally the day came. When workers removed the casket from the ground, they opened it and were shocked to find that Annie's body had turned to stone! An unknown author recorded the event:

...having lain in the silent grave 1 year, 4 months, and 20 days and seemed to be as solid and firm as she was when first buried! Although she did not look natural, it was the opinion of some that her body was in a state of petrification.

Some people think this is a hoax. You decide for yourself.

The Haunting of Alabama

PICKENS COUNTY COURTHOUSE • CARROLLTON

When the Pickens County Courthouse burned down, everyone blamed former slave Henry Wells. Despite the fact that no one really knew who set the fire, Wells was arrested and held in the attic of a building that was to become the new courthouse. One afternoon in February 1878, a lynch mob gathered in front of the new courthouse and demanded that Wells be turned over to them. As Wells peered out a window at the crowd below, a sudden violent rainstorm erupted. A lightning bolt struck nearby, etching Well's terrified expression into the windowpane. Years of scrubbing with every cleaner imaginable has been unable to erase the image. It can still be seen in the lower right-hand windowpane of the new courthouse.

THE PLANTATION HOUSE • PRATTVILLE

Blowing in ears seems to be a favorite ghostly pastime. The Plantation House in Prattville is said to be haunted by a Mr. Davis, a former owner who killed himself in the 1920s. He's a flirty ghost who blows in the ears and touches the backs of female visitors.

SHELL MOUND PARK • DAUPHIN ISLAND

Deep in Shell Mound Park lies a clearing circled by trees, which was once a ceremony site for Native American burials. At night women in native garb can be seen dancing to the sound of drums.

SLOSS FURNACE • BIRMINGHAM

Today, Sloss Furnace is a national historic landmark, but for ninety years after its opening in 1882, it was one of the country's major iron producers. (Alabama is the only place on the planet where all three components of steel-making—iron ore, coal and limestone—are found within a thirty-mile radius.) The massive furnaces with their tons of melted steel were dangerous places to work, and many men lost their lives there. It's no wonder that there are numerous reports of hauntings. One such report is the sighting of worker Theophilus Calvin Jowers, who fell into the Alice Furnace in 1887, while trying to replace the furnace bell. He is often seen on the catwalks above the main floor.

The reports of ghostly happenings are so numerous in Alabama that we even have our own paranormal investigative team to check them out. Called the Alabama Foundation for Paranormal Research, this group sends a team to scientifically investigate and report on supernatural events throughout the Southeast.

TINKER PLACE • GREENSBORO

The spirit of Susian Truman Tinker is said to haunt the halls of Tinker Place, the home built for her. There have been numerous reports of a woman dressed in gray wandering around the mansion and warming her hands at the fireplace. She's also been known to turn on lights upon request.

The Haunting of Alabama

TOMBSTONE OF NANCY DOLLAR • MENTONE

After resident Nancy Dollar and her beloved dog, Buster, died, thieves broke into Dollar's home and stole the money she was saving for her tombstone. Shortly after her burial, the apparition of an old woman was seen walking near the falls. After many sightings, residents took up a collection and erected a tombstone for Miss Dollar. The apparition has not been seen since, although many have claimed to see a phantom dog hanging around her cabin.

UNIVERSITY OF MONTEVALLO'S STUDENT GHOST • MONTEVALLO

Legend has it that the University of Montevallo is haunted by a hapless student who, in the early twentieth century, was heating hot chocolate on a kerosene burner in her dorm room. She spilled some kerosene on her nightgown and was set ablaze. Though her roommate tried to put out the flames with a rug, the girl burned to death as she ran down the hallway. Today, there are reports of an apparition of a girl running down the hallway in a flaming nightgown. In addition, her image is supposedly burned into the dorm room door, despite the fact that the door has been replaced since the incident.

WILLIAM GIBSON'S GRAVE • SPRINGVILLE

You probably won't recognize the name of William Gibson because he did anything notable in his lifetime. No, it's his death that has brought him attention. In particular, his burial. You see, his grave is in a most unusual place. It's right in the corner of

Reable Pearson's yard in Springville on Highway 11. It's not in a cemetery, not even in a family plot. It's just in her yard, alone.

Gibson has been buried there since 1827; a stone says he died on October 20 of that year. But no one knows why he died, or why he was buried so close to the road. A fairly recent history of Springville says he was a hat salesman from North Carolina who camped near the highway, which was once the old Georgia-Tuscaloosa wagon trail. Those who know about the grave say Gibson may have died of disease, but still they don't know why he was buried so near the road. Other, more colorful, stories say Gibson was the victim of a duel, and others say he was gored to death by an ox. Another account suggests that there's even treasure buried nearby.

Either way, he's been in Reable Pearson's yard since before it was Reable Pearson's yard. She keeps the grave clean and sometimes plants flowers, figuring it's the right thing to do.

In the Clayton City Cemetery, a tombstone in the shape of a whiskey bottle marks the grave of William T. Mullen, who died in 1863. It seems Mrs. Mullen, angered by her husband's drinking, threatened him with this posthumous humiliation if he didn't stop drinking. Guess he didn't.

Located on North Midway Street.

Weird Happenings

Hairy men traipsing around the countryside. Spacemen covered in aluminum foil. Fishy rain. Stars falling from the heavens. There are weird things happenin' here.

Big Foot • Clanton

There's a hairy creature inhabiting the woods around Clanton, and no, it's not Uncle Buddy off on a toot. This creature, Alabama's own Big Foot, is more hirsute than your Aunt Thelma and just about as tall (only 4 feet). His nickname is a bit of a misnomer, however, for his feet are normal size. Thing is, they look more like hands than feet.

Leave it to Alabama to put a twist on the legendary creature. According to Big Foot researchers around the country, our Southern Big Foot is unique in that it resembles a chimpanzee instead of the traditional human-ape creature of the North. Experts were excited by the sighting because it "proved" that the Southern Big Foot was much more like an ape than a human.

According to reports, Big Foot was first seen in the fall of 1960 as he trudged through a peach orchard off U.S. Highway 31, just south of Clanton. The sighting was investigated by then-sheriff T.J. Lockhart and his deputy, James Earl Johnson, who described the prints left behind as "the strangest things I ever seen."

The officers made concrete molds of the prints. Those molds were on display until August 2002, when someone in the Sheriff's Department threw them away.

Weird Happenings

There have been no more sightings around Chilton County since that time. However, there were sightings in other areas of the state in 1976 and 1978.

HODGES METEORITE • SYLACAUGA/TUSCALOOSA

On the night of November 30, 1954, Ann Hodges was sitting on her couch, peacefully listening to her radio, when an 8½-pound meteor crashed through the roof and landed on her hip. She was not seriously injured, but Hodges is the only human to ever be hit by a falling star. The

In 1954, Ann Hodges of Sylacauga was struck by a meteorite while sitting on her couch. She received no serious injuries, and the Sylacauga Aerolite is on display at the Museum of Natural History at the University of Alabama.
Courtesy of the University of Alabama
Museum of Natural History

meteorite, officially known as the Sylacauga Aerolite, is on display at the Museum of Natural History, located in Smith Hall on the University of Alabama campus in Tuscaloosa. A replica of the famous meteorite, which has drawn visitors from around the world, is on display at the Comer Museum in Sylacauga.

Forget San Franciso. The first citywide electric trolley was built in Montgomery in 1886.

Jesus Door • Jasper

Many people believe that Jesus is with them everywhere, all the time, but one Walker County father found this to be particularly true as he walked the halls of the local hospital in April of 1983. His son, undergoing surgery following a motorcycle wreck, was in critical condition. As the father paced and looked around in desperation, he noticed what appeared to be eyes in the wood grain pattern of the nearby door. As he continued to pray for his son, he recognized an entire face in the door, which he believed to be the face of Jesus. He took comfort in the image, taking it to be a good sign for his son. Sure enough, word came that the son was stable. He was later transferred to University Hospital and has since recovered.

Word soon spread about the face in the door, and people lined up to see the miraculous image. All in all, about 34,000 people have seen it, including representatives from major television networks.

The door still hangs in Walker Baptist Medical Center on Highway 78 in Jasper, though it has appropriately been moved to the entrance of the second floor prayer room.

Raining catfish • Uniontown

On a clear April day in 1956, a farmer and his wife saw a dark cloud forming in the distance. The cloud moved overhead, and suddenly it began raining, but not cats and dogs. Not in Alabama! This cloud was raining catfish. And bass. And bream. The fish fall lasted about fifteen minutes, during which time the live fish pelted to the ground, flopping around and smelling pretty fishy. The cloud dispersed and once again the sky was clear and bright. Hmmm…. Makes you wonder!

SPACESHIP LANDING • FALKVILLE

On October 17, 1973, the small town of Falkville had visitors from up North … waaay up North. A woman reported to police chief Jeff Greenhaw that a spaceship had landed in a field outside of town. Greenhaw grabbed his camera and headed out to the field, but, alas, there was no spaceship to be found.

While Greenhaw was searching the area, he was startled to see a stranger standing on the roadside. But this was no ordinary stranger. This guy looked like he was wrapped in aluminum foil. He was bright and shiny, and his head and neck appeared to be "made together," Greenhaw said. And an antenna was attached to his head. Definitely not your typical Alabamian. Greenhaw had the presence of mind to snap a few shots with his trusty Polaroid before the stranger took off across a field. Greenhaw pursued in his truck, but because of the rough terrain, he was able to reach a speed of only 35 mph, which the foiled fellow easily outran. "He was running faster than any human I ever saw," Greenhaw said. The stranger disappeared into the forest, never to be seen again.

Despite his photographic "proof," Greenhaw was ridiculed by the townspeople for his belief that Falkville had truly been visited by aliens from outer space. A string of bad luck followed. First, his house burned. Then his wife left him, and he was fired by the town council. Rumor has it that his last investigation was of the great Reynold's Wrap shortage in Falkville.

STARS FELL ON ALABAMA • STATEWIDE

Ever wonder why the state license plate has the phrase Stars Fell On Alabama? It's because stars did, indeed, fall on Alabama. On November 12, 1833, a meteor shower of unprecedented proportions occurred. Thousands of stars plummeted to Earth, setting the Alabama sky ablaze, awing many and frightening others who believed Judgment Day was nigh. Across the state, folks repented their wicked ways, renouncing all manner of sin from drinking and smoking to dancing and gambling.

But, of course, Judgment Day did not come, and wicked ways have made a remarkable comeback. The meteor shower became known as "the night stars fell on Alabama" and has been memorialized in song and on our car tags.

UFO SIGHTING • SOMEWHERE OVER MONTGOMERY

The second ever UFO sighting occurred in 1948, almost 5,000 feet over Alabama. On July 24, on a flight from Houston to Atlanta, Eastern Airline pilots Captain Clarence Chiles and John Whitted saw a strange glowing object coming toward them out of a distant squall. They at first thought it was a jet whose exhaust was glowing against the clouds. But as the object passed off their starboard side, they saw it had no wings. Both men reported seeing rows of brightly glowing windows down the length of the cigar-shaped object. Along its underside was a blue glow and an orange-red exhaust shot from the rear. It was about the length of a B-29 and twice as thick. As it passed, their plane seemed to rock as if hit by a wake. Both men reported seeing the object come to an abrupt stop, and Whitted, who was on the right side, reported that the object suddenly disappeared after a fast vertical ascent.

The pilots checked to see if any passengers could confirm their account, but the only passenger not asleep had a limited view through a small window. Still, he agreed that the sight had been "not like anything I had ever seen."

THE VIRGIN MARY • STERRETT

The Virgin Mary is a regular visitor to this small town in Alabama. She made her first appearance in 1988, when Marija Lunetti of Yugoslavia came to donate a kidney to her brother at UAB Hospital. Ms. Lunetti was one of six children already famous for Virgin Mary sightings seven years earlier in their hometown of Medjugorje, Yugoslavia.

People flocked to the farm where Lunetti was staying in hopes of another visit. They were not disappointed, for Lunetti claims to be visited by the Virgin Mary daily.

Lunetti has returned to this humble field every few years, and always the Virgin Mary has joined her there. News of the sightings has grown, and in 2004, thousands of people from around the world made the pilgrimage to the tiny town of Sterrett, choking the roadways with their cars and overwhelming motels and restaurants. On this visit, as always, the Virgin appeared to Lunetti with her arms outstretched over the field, and when asked for a blessing, she made the sign of the cross over the crowd. Many reported being healed. Others were just thankful to find a parking spot.

Alabama Creature Feature

We're pretty sentimental about our animals here, in the hunting and fishing capital of the South, but it's not just the "normal" pets we form attachments to.

ALABAMA ANIMAL HALL OF FAME • MONTGOMERY

Did you know Alabama has an Animal Hall of Fame? Well, we do. Begun in 2003, the Alabama Animal Hall of Fame is sponsored by the Alabama Veterinary Medical Foundation. It recognizes special animals from around the state. Rockford's Fred, whose story is told later, is there. Another honoree is Red Dog, a bloodhound who works for the St. Clair County Correctional Facility. Red Dog is a crime stopper extraordinaire, having tracked down more than seventeen

Red Dog, the criminal tracker extraordinaire, is honored at the Alabama Animal Hall of Fame, which recognizes the bravery, service, and loyalty of Alabama's special pets.

criminals, including a man who kidnapped a 13-year-old girl. Red Dog tracked him right up to his trailer door.

The Animal Hall of Fame was founded "to celebrate the enduring bond between man and domesticated animals by

recognizing the rare accomplishments that bond produces."
Uh-huh. Just means we like our pets.

The animals honored aren't just your everyday pets, though. These are Alabama animals that have displayed outstanding loyalty, courage, service, or intuitive abilities in their relations with humans. They are nominated by veterinarians, The Humane Society, the Society for the Prevention of Cruelty to Animals, or other animal care agencies.

BLUEGRASS FARMS WILDLIFE SANCTUARY • ATTALLA

Lions and tigers and bears! And wolves! Oh, my! The Bluegrass Farms Wildlife Sanctuary is a retirement home for exotic animals. Founders Ty and Hope Harris are dedicated to rescuing these animals and giving them a peaceful place to live out their lives.

You can visit this peaceable kingdom on Dekalb County Road 345.

COON DOG MEMORIAL GRAVEYARD • CHEROKEE

Coon hunters become especially attached to their dogs, as evidenced by the Coon Dog Memorial Graveyard, located outside of Cherokee.

The cemetery was founded on September 4, 1937, when owner Key Underwood buried Troop, his favorite hunting dog, at his favorite hunting site. Since that time, more and more dogs have been buried there, many marked by gravestones with intricately carved sculptures of dogs treeing coons.

Located south of Cherokee via Colbert County Route 21.

FRED, THE TOWN DOG'S GRAVE • ROCKFORD

Fred was a dog with his own town. The scruffy Airedale mix wandered into the town of Rockford in 1993. He was sick and undernourished. Kind residents nursed him back to health, and in appreciation, Fred adopted Rockford and its residents.

After Fred, an undernourished dog, wandered into the town of Rockford in 1993, he was adopted as the town dog and soon became their most famous resident. Until Fred's death in 2002, the town sign read, "Welcome to Rockford. Home to Fred, the Town Dog."

In the ten years the friendly mutt resided there, he wandered freely around town, meeting and greeting friends and strangers alike. He became the town's most famous resident with his own weekly newspaper column called "A Dog's Life," a line of souvenirs, and his own bank account. His special brand of hospitality was recognized on the town sign: Welcome to Rockford. Home of Fred, the Town Dog. He gained national fame when he was profiled on the cable network Animal Planet.

On December 23, 2002, Fred passed away in a Birmingham animal hospital, the victim of a mysterious animal bite. He was buried behind the Old Rock Jail in Rockford. A full-size gravestone marks his grave.

Alabama Creature Feature

Though the town sign no longer mentions Fred, he will not be forgotten. He was inducted into the Alabama Animal Hall of Fame in 2004.

HARMONY PARK SAFARI • HUNTSVILLE

Who would have thought that in Alabama you could see free-roaming exotic and endangered wildlife, but you can at this federally licensed nature preserve in our own backyard. Stay in your car for the two-mile drive that offers up close and personal sightings of zebras, buffalo, camels, ostriches, pythons, rams, alligators, and water fowl.

Located at 431 Clouds Cove Road in Huntsville.

The state saltwater fish is the fighting tarpon. The state freshwater fish is the largemouth bass.

LEROY BROWN • EUFAULA

Leroy Brown was a largemouth bass caught by the legendary fisherman Tom Mann in 1973. From the moment Leroy bit into Mann's special-made strawberry jelly worm, Mann knew he was no ordinary bass. This fish had spunk. He had personality. Instead of serving the fish for supper, Mann put him in the bass-breeding tank in his bait shop and named him Leroy. Mann developed a strong affection for the fish. He cut a hole in his office and moved the tank so that he could watch Leroy for hours.

Mann's reputation as a fisherman grew, and he turned his bait shop into Tom Mann's Fish World, a mixture of museum and fish/bait shop. One of the main attractions was Leroy, who now lived in a 38-gallon aquarium. During the eight years he lived there, Leroy became the most famous fish in America. When he died of old age in 1981, the governor sent condolences. More than 800 mourners attended his funeral, where they dropped strawberry jelly worms into the casket and the Eufaula High School band played "Bad, Bad Leroy Brown." The pallbearers were bass fishing greats from around the country.

Unfortunately, on the night of the funeral, someone kidnapped Leroy and his casket. The bass-fishing world searched around the globe for the missing Leroy. Finally, three weeks later, a baggage handler in the Tulsa, Oklahoma airport noticed a funky smell coming from a fish-sized package. Sure enough, it was Leroy, quite decomposed at that point.

Mann erected a marble statue of Leroy that bears the inscription: "Most bass are just fish, but Leroy Brown was something special." Leroy's memorial is still located on U.S. Highway 431, though Mann's Fish World was closed after Mann passed away in 2005.

Alabama Creature Feature

The official state reptile is the Alabama red-bellied turtle. This turtle inhabits the fresh and brackish waters of the Mobile Delta in Mobile and Baldwin counties. It is found nowhere else in the world.

Eat, Drink, And Be Merry!

Eating out in Strange But True Alabama is more than a meal—it's an experience. There are restaurants and bars galore along our back roads trail—some historic, some wild, and some just plain fun.

THE BRIGHT STAR RESTAURANT • BESSEMER

The Bright Star Restaurant is a bright star in Alabama's culinary world. Opened in 1907 as a small café with just a horseshoe-shaped bar, the restaurant underwent several growth spurts—owing mainly to Bessemer's place as a booming steel town. In 1915, the Bright Star moved to its present location and introduced patrons

The historic Bright Star Restaurant in Bessemer is known around the Southeast for its steak and seafood and for its Victorian-style décor.
Courtesy of Bright Star Restaurant

to a new dining experience, featuring crystal chandeliers and white tablecloths. Ceiling fans, tile floors, and mirrored and marbled walls, most of which are there today, reflected the style of the era. Murals painted by a traveling European artist are another interesting feature of the Victorian-style décor.

The history and atmosphere is not the Bright Star's main attraction, however. The food—seafood and steaks made with a Greek flair—is known throughout the Southeast. Over the last ten years, the restaurant has consistently been ranked among the top three restaurants in Birmingham. Additionally, the Bright Star was recognized in the *U.S. Congressional Record* in 1966 for its status as an Alabama landmark and its service to the community.

The Bright Star is located at 304 Nineteenth Street North.

EZELL'S FISH CAMP • LAVACA

Ezell's Fish Camp is more than a restaurant. It's a cultural icon. Located on the Tombigbee River, the original building dates back to the time of the Civil War, when it served as a trading post. In the late 1920s, then-owner C.A. Ezell, a commercial fisherman, began using the building to house his hunting club. He had his cook prepare meals for the group and for private parties held there. By the 1950s, Ezell's hunting club dinners had evolved into a full-time restaurant, with fresh, fried catfish as the main dish.

Not a lot has changed in the last fifty years. You still drive through the middle of a cotton field to get to the rustic restaurant-cabin. There are rocking chairs on the front porch, and the animals mounted everywhere remind you of the building's origins. If you're not squeamish, take a gander at a shadowbox that displays rattlesnake tails, and tails and claws of various local creatures—presumably, none of which have been served as supper! Ezell's is still popular with hunters, and the restaurant regularly hosts family and class reunions, political dinners, high school events, and religious events.

Today, the catfish is pond-raised, fried just right, and served with sweet coleslaw, hushpuppies, and fresh-cut French fries. Oh, and a giant glass of sweet iced tea. If catfish ain't to your liking, don't despair. Ezell's also offers steaks, hamburgers, chicken, and seafood. There are even a few specialty items, such as fried dill pickles and frog legs.

Located off Highway 10, east of Lavaca.

THE FLORA-BAMA LOUNGE • GULF SHORES

Located on the Alabama/Florida line, the Flora-Bama Lounge is probably the state's most famous—and craziest—bar. Opened in 1961 as a hole-in-the-wall dive, the Flora-Bama has remained popular until its demise on September 16, 2004, when Hurricane Ivan paid a visit.

But don't worry, it didn't stay down for long. It was soon back in full swing.

And why not? This quintessential beach bar was perched precariously on the sparkling blue Gulf and had everything for the discerning reveler: three band stages, ten bars, an oyster bar, a large fenced-in party area, beach volleyball courts, a package store, and even a recording studio.

And it wasn't just the accommodations that made the Flora-Bama so popular. It was also the laid-back, beach attitude that permeated the atmosphere and spurred a multitude of strange goings-on.

Consider, if you will:

- The Polar Bear Dip in the Gulf. January 1, 2005, marked the twentieth anniversary of this strange ritual. Crazy people gather at the Flora-Bama, strip to their swimsuits or maybe even their birthday suits, and take a plunge into the frigid Gulf.

- The Easter Bunny Drop and Egg Hunt, where the Easter Bunny parachutes down to the bar and hides more than 3,000 of his little eggs up and down the beach for partygoers to find.

- The Mullet Man Triathlon, with categories such as the Athena, for women 145 pounds or more, The Clydesdale and Super Clydesdale for men 200 pounds or more, and the Fat Tire for men and women riding fat-tire bicycles.

- The Interstate Mullet Toss. Held annually on the last Friday in April, this competition draws hundreds of competitors to see who can throw a dead mullet the farthest distance over the Alabama state line. Thousands of partiers come from around the country to watch.

- The Miss Firecracker Bikini Contest. OK, that one is pretty much expected of a beach bar.

Alabama's state fruit is the blackberry. The state nut is the pecan.

LAMBERT'S CAFÉ • FOLEY

Lambert's Café. Home of the Throwed Roll. Forget what Mom said. In this restaurant, it's OK to throw food—the rolls, anyway. When the rolls come out of the oven, waiters announce "Fresh, Hot Rolls!" If you want one, raise your hand, and it'll be thrown to you—from across the room. The tradition packs customers from around the globe to this café—and trains quite a few good pitchers. It's rumored that Nolan Ryan got his start here.

Lambert's is located eight miles north of Gulf Shores, on S. McKenzie.

MANCI'S ANTIQUE CLUB • DAPHNE

L.A. (Lower Alabama) seems to be a hot spot for fun bars. In this small town on the eastern shore of Mobile Bay, you'll find Manci's Antique Club, a combination bar/museum. First opened as a gas station in 1924 by the Manci family, the building was converted in 1967. Now run by a third-generation family member, the bar exhibits collections of antique tools, Native American artifacts, Victrolas, rickshaws, and an exceedingly large display of Jim Beam decanters. The bar claims to be "The Bloody Mary Capital of the Eastern Shore" and has a sign that always promises Free Beer Tomorrow.

Located at the corner of Daphne and Belrose Avenues.

THE ORIGINAL WHISTLESTOP CAFÉ • IRONDALE

Another historic restaurant is the Irondale Café, now also known as The Original WhistleStop Café. Opened in 1928 as a hotdog stand, the little café underwent several incarnations before being bought by Bess Fortenberry, great-aunt of TV star and author Fannie Flagg, who made the restaurant the setting for her novel *Fried Green Tomatoes* at the WhistleStop Café.

The restaurant changed hands after Fortenberry suffered a stroke in 1972 and has grown from a seating capacity of thirty-two to 260. The food hasn't changed, though. The restaurant is well known for its down-home cooking—black-eyed peas, homemade squash casserole, turnip greens, and of course, that uniquely Southern culinary delight—fried green tomatoes.

The Irondale Café is located at 1906 First Avenue North.

PINK PONY PUB • GULF SHORES

The world famous Pink Pony Pub. Another beach bar, the Pink Pony serves up food, drink, and fun in a tropical atmosphere. You can't miss it. It's the bright pink building located right on the beach at Gulf Shores.

RED'S LITTLE SCHOOL HOUSE • GRADY

Red's Little School House is a restaurant housed in a former schoolhouse. It serves an all-you-can-eat buffet of fresh home-cooked vegetables—so fresh they were grown on the premises by co-owner Red Deese. The school's original chalkboards, old maps, and president's portraits might remind you of eating in the school cafeteria, except that the food's too good. Chef Debbie Deese has cooked for three governors and one president.

Located at 20 Gardner Road.

SLICK LIZARD SMOKE HOUSE • NAUVOO

Why would anyone name a restaurant the Slick Lizard
Smoke House? Well, it's named for a local coal mine located
behind the café. The mine supposedly got its name when one
coal miner said to another as they were crawling from the mine
(in those days, mining was done crawling through slick clay
openings just 25 inches high), "You're slick as a lizard." The
restaurant's owner invites customers to "come fill your gizzard
at Slick Lizard!"

Located at 7146 Nauvoo Road.

Alabama has an official state biscuit. Former Governor
Fob James declared the biscuits of the late Eunice Merrell,
who ran Eunice's Country Kitchen in Huntsville for more
than fifty years, "the best in Alabama." His proclamation
made her biscuits the official state biscuits. They also were
mentioned in a tribute in the *U.S. Congressional Record*.
Aunt Eunice, as she was affectionately called by most,
died in February 2004.

Miscellaneous Miscellany

More points of strangeness along the Strange But True Alabama trail.

It's The Law!

Better watch your step in our Strange But True Alabama. You never know when the long arm of the law may reach out and nab you for breaking some of these strange but true laws!

1. It's illegal for a driver to be blindfolded while operating a vehicle in Alabama. Makes it difficult to see all those neat roadside attractions, too.

2. It's legal to drive the wrong way down a one-way street in Lee County if you have a lantern attached to the front of your vehicle. So, put the lantern on and head out!

3. You must have windshield wipers on your car. Even if it's not raining.

4. Dominoes cannot be played on Sunday. OK, not a problem.

5. It's illegal to have an ice cream cone in your back pocket at anytime. 'Nuff said.

6. It is illegal to wear a fake mustache that causes laughter in church. Everyone knows that giggling in church is a big no-no!

7. It's illegal to wear women's pumps with sharp, high heels in Mobile. That's especially true for you guys.

8. Men may not spit in front of the opposite sex. Didn't your mother teach you better than that?

9. It's illegal to drive barefooted in Alabama. Bet that one's broken a lot!

The longest jail sentence ever passed in the United States was meted out to Dudley Wayne Kyzer by a court in Tuscaloosa. In 1981, Kyzer received 10,000 years for murdering his wife. He then was sentenced to two life terms for murdering his mother-in-law and a college student. However, he became eligible for parole only ten years later. He has not received parole to date.

10. It's illegal to maim oneself to escape duty. Sounds a bit drastic just to get some time off!

11. In Headland, no female wearing a nightgown can be taken on a private plane. She can't fly on one either.

12. It's a felony in Alabama to cut off your arm to make people feel sorry for you and give you money. Hmmm, makes you wonder!

13. No mules can be traded after supper when the sun has already gone below the horizon. So, trade early and eat late.

14. In Tuscumbia, no more than eight rabbits can reside on the same block. Well, officer, I just had two. Then, I turned my back for just a minute ...

15. Putting salt on a railroad track is punishable by death in this state, so don't do it.

16. In Anniston, it's illegal to wear blue jeans down Noble Street.

17. In Mobile, it's illegal to howl at ladies within the city limits. Must be a lot of wolves in Baldwin County!

18. In Alabama, it's illegal to flick boogers into the wind. Not a good idea to flick them against the wind either.

19. Bathing in public fountains is prohibited in Mobile. The water gets all soapy!

20. In Mobile, it's illegal for pigeons to eat pebbles from composite roofs. Officer, arrest that bird!

Strange Town Names

The laws in some of our towns and counties aren't the only thing strange. How about some of the names of the towns and how they came to be?

BUG TUSSLE • CULLMAN COUNTY

This town was previously named Wilburn, but was changed to Bug Tussle thanks to a lover of white lightning, Charlie

Miscellaneous Miscellany

Campbell. One day as Campbell indulged in his favorite brew, he became fascinated by watching two tumble bugs trying to roll a ball of dirt across the road. He told people the bugs appeared to be tussling. The expression caught on, and the community came to be called Bug Tussle.

BURNT CORN • MONROE AND CONECUH COUNTIES

Opinions differ on how this small community got its name. One account says that white settlers burned the corn fields of the Creek Indians to clear land for homesteads. Others believe it was the Indians that burned the fields of the white man. Still others claim the name came from a story about a group of Indians traveling from Pensacola to the Upper Creek Nation who were forced to leave an ailing companion by a stream with only a supply of corn. When he recovered, he had no way to carry the leftover corn, so it was eventually burned in his campfire. People who camped there later said that they camped where the "corn had burnt." Whichever story is correct, they are all colorful possibilities.

The web site of this farming community boasts a population of 300 residents within its five square miles, divided between Monroe and Conecuh counties. Places of interest include numerous historic buildings, one of which is a casket warehouse.

ECLECTIC • ELMORE COUNTY

To most people, eclectic means "employing elements from a variety of sources." But to Dr. Thomas Fielder, an 1840s resident of what came to be Eclectic, the word meant "that which is best." He felt that this definition aptly described his course of study in school and named his town accordingly.

EQUALITY • COOSA COUNTY

This community of about one hundred people got its name because of its location at the exact center of the 36-mile route from Wetumpka to Kellyton.

Equality was originally called Brooksville, but the name had to be changed when the post office was established in 1849 because a Brooksville already existed in Alabama. The equal distance between the Wetumpka and Kellyton post offices suggested the replacement name.

INTERCOURSE • SUMTER COUNTY

Whew! Try Googling this town! You'll get quite an education! But the real story is pretty tame: Intercourse is named for a crossroads where the general store is located. According to legend, a sign posted outside the town's meeting hall had to be removed after there were several car crashes at the intersection. The sign read Intercourse Lessons Wednesday Night.

LICKSKILLET • DEKALB COUNTY

Some people say that this town got its name because folks here were once so poor they had to lick their frying pans for nourishment. But it really got its name from a phrase about the local ball team in the late 1800s and early 1900s. After the games, residents would head to the local store, and when someone would ask who won the game, the winner would always respond, "We licked their skillet."

PHIL CAMPBELL • FRANKLIN COUNTY

This community enjoys the distinction of being the first city or town in Alabama to be named after an individual using both the first and last names. In the 1880s, a railroad company was laying track from Florence to Birmingham, and the rail lines passed through the area. A local landowner contacted the rail's project engineer and promised that if a sidetrack and depot were laid adjacent to his land, any community arising around them would be named for the project engineer. Well, the sidetrack was laid. The depot was built, and a community soon surrounded it. In 1911, the town was officially incorporated and named for the project engineer—Phil Campbell.

POSSUM BEND • WILCOX COUNTY

This small community on the Alabama River got its name from a nineteenth century riverboat pilot, Jerimiah Austell. On his trips up and down the river, he would get off his boat at Buford Landing to see his girlfriend. The name of Possum Bend came from the possums Austell saw at the river's bend as he walked to the next landing to catch up with his boat the next morning.

REMLAP • BLOUNT COUNTY

Rumor has it that this Blount County town was so named in a fit of pique by its founder, who was upset at his brother. It seems his brother, too, had founded a town just down the highway. In naming his town Palmerdale, he had laid claim to the family name. Determined not to be outdone, the second brother used the family name as well—spelled backwards.

SCANT CITY • MARSHALL COUNTY

During the 1800s, the mountain moonshiners in this area sold their whiskey in scant pints. So the area took on the name of Scant City.

SCRATCH ANKLE • MONROE COUNTY

This bump on the map got its name because of the prolific mosquito population. Scratching seemed to be the main pastime here.

Ever wonder why Alabama is called the Heart of Dixie? It comes from the $10 notes issued by the Citizens Bank of Louisiana before the Civil War. The notes bore the word "dix," the French word for ten, and the South became known as Dixieland. As everyone knows, Alabama is smack dab in the middle of Dixie—at its very heart!

SLAPOUT • ELMORE COUNTY

One legend has it that this town, also known as Holtville-Slapout, got its name because the owner of the general store

Miscellaneous Miscellany

would often tell customers he was "slap out" of merchandise. We think a better explanation is that the town used to be "slap out" in the middle of nowhere.

Located eighteen miles outside of Montgomery.

SMUT EYE • BULLOCK COUNTY

Though it was originally named "Welcome," the current name of this rural community is a reminder of the smut blown from the bellows in the blacksmith shop of George Pope, who was often so covered with smut that all you could see were his eyes. The smut collected on all those who worked on or near them. People came to call the shop "smut eye" and then came to call the community that as well.

Located on Highway 239 and County Road 14, about twelve miles south of Union Springs.

THREE NOTCH • BULLOCK COUNTY

Before the Civil War, General Andrew Jackson ordered his troops south from Fort Mitchell on the Chattahoochee River all the way to Pensacola. Their job was to cut a route for transporting troops and supplies. They marked their trail by cutting three notches into trees as they went. The community got its name from that practice.

TOADVINE • JEFFERSON COUNTY

You might think this name came from something creepy and crawly, but the story actually has to do with a person that bore that name.

When the War Between the States began in 1861, Cape Smith, son of one of the early settlers in this community, marched proudly with a Jefferson County unit to the battle front. Brave as he was, he nonetheless fell into the hands of federal soldiers, who learned immediately that he had a nervous temperament. In particular, whistling annoyed him.

A fellow prisoner named Nash, a large man, took every opportunity to exploit this weakness. Since Smith was a small, timid man, he was no physical match for his tormentor, and his requests for Nash to stop whistling were ignored. However, a third prisoner named Toadvine took on Smith's cause and struck Nash in the face. Nash rose to fight, but Toadvine won, and the whistling stopped.

When Smith returned home, a post office was established in the new community, and Smith suggested that the area be named in honor of his friend, Toadvine. The name was adopted and remains until this day twenty-five miles west of Birmingham, within six miles of the Warrior River.

TRICKEM • CLEBURNE COUNTY

When three communities in Cleburne County merged into one town, it became known as "Tri-Com." Unfortunately, the name got mispronounced as "trick 'em," hence the current name.

Towns of Note

ALBERTVILLE • MARSHALL COUNTY

This tiny town located in the heart of Sand Mountain is known to firefighters around the world as "The Fire Hydrant

Capital of the World." Mueller Company, a major producer of fire hydrants, has called this Marshall County town home since 1975, though it has made hydrants since 1934.

CHILDERSBURG • TALLADEGA COUNTY

The tiny town of Albertville is home to the Mueller Company, a major producer of fire hydrants and is known as "The Fire Hydrant Capital of the World."
Courtesy of Amber K. Henderson

The good people of Florida claim St. Augustine to be the oldest city in the country, but they are sadly mistaken. Childersburg is known as the oldest continually occupied city in the United States. According to the *Final Report of the United States DeSoto Expedition Commission*, Hernando de Soto visited Childersburg in 1540, many years before the 1565 founding of St. Augustine. A description of DeSoto Caverns, then known as Kymulga Cave, was found in the records of the time. This natural wonder is included in an earlier chapter of our book as well.

FORT PAYNE • DEKALB COUNTY

Stuff a sock in it! Thanks to the many sock mills located here, Fort Payne is the world's largest sock producers and is designated as "The Sock Capital of the World." According to the National Association of Hosiery Manufacturers, one out of every eight people in the United States is wearing socks from the Fort Payne/DeKalb County area on any given day. More than 12 million pairs of socks are shipped from here every week. That's a lot of socks!

GADSDEN • ETOWAH COUNTY

Where the rubber meets the road. Gadsden is home to the Goodyear Tire and Rubber Company, which established the rubber industry in the South when it opened here in 1928. It is the oldest plant in North America.

GEE'S BEND • WILCOX COUNTY

Gee's Bend is a small rural community settled on a horseshoe-shaped bend on the Alabama River, southwest of Selma. Founded in antebellum times, it was the site of cotton plantations, the largest of which was owned by Joseph Gee and later by Mark Pettway, who bought Gee's plantation in 1850. After the Civil War, the freed slaves stayed on as tenant farmers and took the surname of Pettway. Gee's Bend became an African-American village. Many of today's residents are direct descendents of these original slaves and still bear the Pettway surname.

Cut off from surrounding communities on three sides by the Alabama River, the inhabitants of Gee's Bend were left mostly to themselves for almost one hundred years after the end of the Civil War, and many of the community's folkways and traditions survived untouched well into the twentieth century.

One of these traditions—quilting—has brought national attention and high praise to Gee's Bend. Many quilts of Gee's Bend, made using traditions handed down from generation to generation, now hang in famous art galleries around the world. The quilt makers, women who've lived in this community all their lives, are the subjects of several magazine articles and television documentaries.

HUNTSVILLE • MADISON COUNTY

The Marshall Space Flight Center rocketed the U.S. into outer space—and turned a one-horse town into Rocket City. Established in 1960, the Space Flight Center was the hub for the country's space exploration program. Then-Director Wernher von Braun and his team of German space flight scientists first developed the Jupiter rocket, used to shoot the first unmanned satellites into space, and the Mercury-Redstone that sent Alan Shepard on the country's first sub-orbital flight. In the 1960s, they began development of the Saturn rockets, particularly the Saturn V, a multi-staged rocket that propelled Apollo 11 to the first moon landing—and five subsequent Apollo moon flights. Other significant milestones include the design and development of the lunar rover vehicle, the development of major components for the construction and

In the 1960s, Wernher von Braun, director of the Space Flight Center, made Huntsville a hub for the country's space explorations program. Today, the Marshall Space Flight Center continues to develop plans for unmanned space missions and space stations.
Courtesy of NASA

launch of the manned space station, Skylab, and the development of the space shuttles.

The Marshall Space Flight Center remains in the forefront of the U.S. space exploration program with extensive plans for more manned space flight vehicles and space stations that promise to take us … where no one has gone before. Beam me up, Scottie!

Magnolia Springs • Baldwin County

Just nine miles from the Gulf in Baldwin County, Magnolia Springs is the only town in the U.S. with an all-water mail route, with daily delivery by boat.

Monroeville • Monroe County

This town, along with Monroe County, has been designated by the Alabama legislature as the "Literary Capital of Alabama." Author Truman Capote grew up in Monroeville, as did writer Harper Lee. The two were good friends, and as children, they spent many hours roaming the streets of Monroeville. No doubt, the town was the main inspiration in Lee's novel *To Kill A Mockingbird*. Other writers who hailed from this area include Mark Childress and Cynthia Tucker.

Montgomery • Montgomery County

Besides being the state capital, Montgomery is noted as being the home of the world's first civilian flying school, established in 1910 by none other than the world's first pilots, Wilbur and Orville Wright. The world's first night flights were

Miscellaneous Miscellany

made here. The Maxwell Air Force Base now occupies the site of this historic school.

MOUNDVILLE • HALE COUNTY

Moundville is the site of an ancient village that was North America's largest city north of Mexico 800 years ago. Occupied by a large settlement of the Mississippian culture from AD 1000 until AD 1450, the community was a 300-acre village built on a bluff overlooking the Black Warrior River. There are twenty-six earthen mounds, the larger of which were the homes of the culture's nobility. Archeologists have uncovered evidence of public buildings, small houses, and burial

In Moundville, a museum houses Native American artifacts, and there are still twenty-six earthen mounds.
Courtesy of Moundville Archaeological Park, University of Alabama

chambers. At its height, Moundville was home to about 1,000 residents, their prosperity supplied by the cultivation of maize. The village is renowned for the skilled workmanship in artifacts of pottery, stonework, and embossed copper. Just like the Mayan culture of South America, Moundville's civilization mysteriously disappeared, with most of the area abandoned by the mid-1500s.

A museum housing the many intricate artifacts was opened in 1939 and remains open to the public. Located on Highway 69, fourteen miles south of Tuscaloosa.

TUXEDO JUNCTION • JEFFERSON COUNTY

You have probably heard of the famous music with this name, but did you know the song was named after a real place in Alabama? Even stranger, it's not a town, not even a small community, simply a turning around point for the Birmingham Trolley Car's Wylam and Pratt City Streetcar. But never mind that, it still provided inspiration for Erskine Hawkins' famous song, "Tuxedo Junction." The tribute to the writer's hometown was wildly popular, eventually coming to the attention of bandleader Glenn Miller, stationed at Maxwell Air Force Base in nearby Montgomery. Miller bought the song, recorded it, and sold 3.5 million copies. It became a favorite tune of U.S. servicemen during the war years.

Nearby, at the intersection of Ensley Avenue and 20th Street, is the Nixon Building, which in its heyday, housed a dancehall on its second floor. For almost thirty years, it was the social hub of the surrounding predominantly black communities.

Many regulars to the dancehall were simple, blue-collar workers by day who loved to dress up and socialize at night. They would leave their jobs at the end of their shifts and return later dressed in their best suits for a night of dancing and dining. Zoot suits were popular, and tuxedos, though most men didn't own the latter. One account of this time in Birmingham's history says that to accommodate men who wanted to leave their jobs and get to the ballroom as soon as possible, a local enterprising businessman started renting tuxedos to the men.

The glory days of Tuxedo Junction are gone, but they are remembered annually with the "Function in the Junction," sponsored by the Erskine Hawkins Foundation and the City of Birmingham. The event pays tribute to a time gone by, to a favorite son that brought national attention to the community he loved, and to the rich music heritage that saw the birth of many notable talents.

"Tuxedo Junction" has been said to be the most widely copied trumpet solo in music history. Birmingham native Wilbur "Dud" Bascomb played the solo on the classic recording.

WETUMPKA • ELMORE COUNTY

The town of Wetumpka is located on the brim of a five-mile-wide meteorite crater. The meteorite crashed to Earth about 83 million years ago.

Wetumpka, an Indian term meaning rumbling waters, has a rich aboriginal history as well. DeSoto reported the presence of a palisade village there built around AD 1000. In 1717, the French established Fort Toulouse as a military outpost and trading center, which was the beginning of an important trade hub for the area.

World Record Holders

Several Alabamians have achieved star status as strange world record holders. Here are just a few:

FASTEST HOMEBUILDING

The fastest Habitat for Humanity house to be built is located in Shelby County's Montevallo. Built by local professionals, not volunteers as is usually the case, the house was erected in 3 hours, 26 minutes, and 34 seconds.

VIDEO GAME WIZARD

Mark Soileau, a native of Florence, is a video game wizard. Soileau scored 155,000 points in the video game *Wizard of War*, a feat that made him the world record holder until recently. He is featured in the *Twin Galaxies' Official Video Game & Pinball Book of World Record*, the official record book for the world of video game and pinball playing. Wonder if there'll be a song about him?

WORLD'S LARGEST CAKE

EarthGrains Bakery and residents of Fort Payne are in the book. According to the *Guinness Book of World Records*, the world's largest cake was baked in Fort Payne on October 18, 1989. The cake weighed 128,238 lbs., 8 oz., which included 16,209 lbs. of icing. Guess that means the residents of Fort Payne could have their cake and ... yeah, yeah, you know.

Miscellaneous Miscellany

WORLD'S YOUNGEST GRADUATE

The University of South Alabama is listed in the *Guinness Book of World Records* for the youngest graduate. Michael Kearney of California graduated with a BA in anthropology at the age of 10 years, 4 months.

Growing Up Alabama

An Alabama childhood is an upbringing rich in language, myths, old home remedies, and folklore. Here are some things that are distinctly ours.

A Language All Our Own

If you're a native Alabamian, no doubt you've heard—and uttered—many of these uniquely Southern sayings.

- After a big supper at Grandma's, you may proclaim yourself to be as *full as a tick.*

- That ole coonhound of yours might be *faster than greased lightnin'.*

- The local car salesman might be *slicker than a greased hog.*

- If you really like something, it's *gooder 'n snuff!*

- Uncle Buddy might be *so buck toothed, he could eat corn-on-the-cob through a keyhole.*

- No doubt about it, those little kittens are *cute as a bug in a rug.*

- Aunt Mattie might be *as nervous as a long-tailed cat in a room full of rockers.*

- After a hard day, you may feel like you were *rode hard and put up wet.*

- Anytime you're feeling sassy, you're *as happy as a dead pig in the sunshine.*

- You might say about a couple of kids that they're *like two peas in a pod.*

- *Well, butter my butt, and call me a biscuit!* No comment on that one.

- You might say about an unattractive fellow that *he fell out of an ugly tree and hit every limb on the way down!*

- On the other hand, the local beauty may be *purtier than a speckled pup.*

- Someone tell a tall tale? Just tell him that *dog won't hunt.*

- And the famous last words of an Alabama redneck: *Hey, ya'll! Watch this!*

Folk Remedies

As surely as kudzu grows in summer, your Meemaw's made you hold your nose and open up for a healthy dose of one of her sure cures.

- If you grew up in Alabama, no doubt you grew up believing that frog pee caused warts. There were many remedies to get rid of the warts you got from handling incontinent frogs, but one stands out: Rub the wart with a piece of raw meat. Bury the meat in the garden. (Of course, you have a garden!) As the meat rots, the wart will slowly fall off.

- Everybody knows about chicken soup for a cold, but unless you're a Southern native, bet you don't know about many weed tea. To make this healing concoction, you gather dried cow patties from the pasture, and place them in cloth along with other ingredients, such as lemons, lavender, and honey. Some people add other herbs as well. Then, you tie the cloth up, and boil the mixture in water. Strain the mixture, add a little sugar if you want, then down it. Supposed to be a sure cure for a cold and pneumonia. Won't do much for that case of nausea, though.

- Got a cut that won't stop bleeding? Snare a few cobwebs with a broom, and apply them to the cut. Guaranteed to stop the bleeding.

- Tobacco juice will take the sting out of bee stings. Know how you get tobacco juice? That's right. Just chew and spit!

- Earwax is good for fever blisters. Ugh!

- Bacon fat taped to embedded glass will draw it out. Watch out; you don't want to lose a finger to that pack of hound dogs following you around, though.

- Grampa's favorite cold remedy is a mixture of tea, honey, lemon juice, and a healthy shot of Wild Turkey whiskey. A couple of those, and you won't care that you're sick. But, whoa! Watch out for that hangover the next day.

- For itching, especially from poison ivy, mix oatmeal into bath water and plunge in. Add a little butter and sugar, and you've got breakfast.

MYTHS

You may even to this day believe some of those tales the grownups told you. Many of the myths in Alabama involve wildlife, especially snakes, perhaps because Alabama has six species of poisonous snakes, including rattlesnakes, coral snakes, cottonmouths, and copperheads. And that doesn't include the twenty-nine species of non-venomous serpents.

- There's an urban legend that's been around for more than fifty years about a young girl who fell into the river and landed in a nest of water moccasins. The girl was bitten numerous times, and, of course, she died. That one scared the bejesus out of anyone living close to the water. However, it never happened. And couldn't happen, since water moccasins are solitary creatures and do not form nests.

- Old folks tell stories of the "hoop snake," a snake that can take its tail in its mouth and roll like a hoop after you.

- There's also stories of the "whipping snake," which can "flail a man to death" with its whip-like tail. This story most likely comes from the coachwhip snake, which is fast and aggressive, but which cannot brandish its tail like a whip.

- More snake lore: Hanging a dead snake belly-up over a barbed wire fence will bring rain.

- Heard the one about snapping turtles and thunder? Legend has it that if a snapping turtle snaps onto you, it won't let go until it thunders. Let's pray for rain!

One of the most famous Alabama legends is the legend of John Henry, the steel-driving man immortalized in lore and in song. According to legend, John Henry worked for Columbus and Western Railroad, driving steel to lay tracks. Henry was well known as the strongest and fastest steel driver around. When the manufacturer of the new steam-powered steel drivers wanted to demonstrate their wares to the bigwigs of the company, John Henry challenged them to a race, hoping to show the bosses that mechanical drivers could never outdo a man.

Many believe this race, held in September 1887, took place at the Oak Mountain Tunnel near Leeds. More than 1,000 spectators gathered to watch John Henry go up against the newfangled machine. The contest lasted for eight hours, and John Henry won, driving his steel rod six feet deeper than the steam driver did. However, the effort proved too much for John Henry's mighty heart. He died there, just outside the east portal of Oak Mountain Tunnel. Legend has it that ten feet of the sixteen-foot steel rod remains embedded in the rock at Oak Mountain Tunnel.

- How about the praying mantis? For generations, children have been terrified of this harmless insect because of its reputed ability to spit in your eyes and blind you. Don't look, Margaret!

For generations, many Alabama children have been told that praying mantises would spit in their eyes and blind them.

- Old folks always tell you that when you kill a snake, be sure to cut off its head. If you don't, it will come alive again—maybe bent on revenge!

- They'll also tell you that if you kill a snake, it won't die until sundown. This may come from the fact that a snake's muscles may twitch for several hours after it has died.

- For generations, grownups have scared their kids with stories about the giant black panther that lives in the deep woods of Alabama. (While the panther is not native to Alabama, the Florida panther is, and rarely, black

Occasionally, the Florida panther or black jaguar will be spotted in Alabama.

jaguars have been spotted in the South.) Its shrill cry, which sounds like a woman screaming, can be heard on dark nights, especially when you're sitting around a campfire.

- Just to set the record straight.... There is no such thing as a glass snake—a snake that breaks into several pieces then puts itself back together—or a water rattler. Rattlesnakes can swim, but they don't live in the water.

OLD WIVES' TALES

Bet you grew up knowing these wisdoms.

- Don't swallow watermelon seeds. They'll grow in your belly!

- Don't let someone sweep under your feet. You'll never get married (or go to jail, as another version says). To break that spell, you must spit on the broom and break it.

- When you clean your comb, don't throw the hair outside. If birds make nests from it, you'll lose your hair.

- Don't point your finger at a graveyard. It'll fall off.

- Don't cut a mole off. You'll bleed to death.

Funny Happenin's Here

Motorcycle mamas, pets dressed up in silly costumes, revelers in the streets, tall-tale tellers, seafood going crazy. ... There's just no end to the funny goings-on in Strange But True Alabama.

ALABAMA TALE TELLIN' FESTIVAL • SELMA

Tall-tale telling is as much a part of Alabama as fried green tomatoes. Several festivals include storytelling in their entertainment, but there's only one where tellin' tales is the only point. The Alabama Tale Tellin' Festival, held in Selma on the second weekend in October, is the brainchild of Alabama's premier storyteller, Kathryn Tucker Windham.

The festival begins Friday evening with a swapping ground, where folks come and share their own tall tales, and then proceeds to tall-tale telling by guest tellers. On Saturday visitors can stroll down historic Water Avenue and shop for crafts and wares from all over the South at Riverfront Market Day. The festival concludes with more tall tales Saturday night. So bring your tales and join in! And so, I says to Bubba, I says, "Bubba, watch this!" An' the next thing I knowed ...

BLESSING OF THE FLEET • BAYOU LA BATRE

If you love seafood, check out the annual Blessing of the Fleet Festival in the fishing community of Bayou La Batre. The festival opens the shrimp season and centers on a parade of

Funny Happenin's Here

The Blessing of the Fleet Festival in Bayou La Batre opens the shrimp season. Decorated boats cruise up the bayou to receive blessing from the Archbishop of St. Margaret's Catholic Church. The festivities include competitions between local seafood restaurants and prizes for the best boat decorations.
Courtesy of J&D Richardson

colorfully decorated boats that cruise up the bayou to receive a blessing from the Archbishop of St. Margaret's Catholic Church. This is an Old World Mediterranean tradition, which offers prayers for abundant catches and protection from the dangers of the sea.

There's also a land parade and contests of all flavors. Prizes are awarded for various categories in boat decoration. And then there are the competitions between local seafood preparers, who compete in picking crabs, shucking oysters, and heading shrimp. Spectators are awed by their speed and by the savory dishes made with the prepared seafood.

Bayou La Batre gained national fame as the site of the fictional Bubba Gump's Shrimp in the movie *Forrest Gump*. Mama always said life is like a pot of gumbo ... a little spicy and full of surprises.

CATFISH FESTIVAL • SCOTTSBORO

Every Alabamian knows the wonder of catfish fried light, served with hushpuppies, French fries, and a big ol' glass of sweet tea. It's no wonder that Alabama ranks second in the nation in catfish sales. And it's no wonder that the town of Scottsboro holds an annual festival celebrating this delectable, bottom-feeding delight. There are catfish rodeos for kids and adults alike, food, and live entertainment.

CHICKEN AND EGG FESTIVAL • MOULTON

Don't miss the Chicken and Egg Festival in Moulton. Held to promote the poultry industry in Lawrence County, the outdoor festival features live entertainment, arts and crafts, a battle of the bands, and food, most of which tastes remarkably like … chicken. There's even a festival mascot named Nugget. Wonder if they'll answer that age-old question … which came first?

Nugget is the mascot of the Chicken and Egg Festival in Moulton. The event, which promotes the poultry industry in Lawrence County, includes a battle of the bands, arts and crafts, and lots of chicken.
Courtesy of the Lawrence County Chamber of Commerce

DO DAH DAY • BIRMINGHAM

Puppies on parade. And kitties. And hamsters. Even iguanas. Birmingham's Do Dah Day is a doggone pet celebration. Held every spring to raise money for animal charity groups and showcase the wonders of pets, this festival features a parade of pets and their humans, many wearing funny costumes, a pet and owner look-alike contest, an Adopt-A-Pet Center, and many other animal-related activities. You won't find any flea circuses here, but there's live music and food—including gourmet treats for the pets. A panting-good time is guaranteed to be had by all. Just remember to watch your step!

DULCIMER & PSALTERY FESTIVALS • McCALLA

For you lovers of obscure music, there's the Southern Appalachian Dulcimer Festival on the first weekend of May and the Down Home Psaltery Festival on the second weekend of June each year. The psaltery festival is the only one of its kind in the country. Imagine that.

Both the psaltery and the dulcimer are stringed instruments that have a rich history in Appalachian folk music. The festivals gather players from around the country to showcase their talents as they compete against other players. There are also workshops for those wanting to learn to play these instruments or to hone their skills. Held at Tannehill Ironworks Historical Park in McCalla.

DUMPLIN' DAYS FESTIVAL • DECATUR

The Dumplin' Days Festival in Decatur features live music, food, a Little Miss Dumplin' pageant, and arts and crafts. Story telling is also a big part of this festival, including a contest for the biggest whopper told.

JUBILEES • MOBILE

Wondering why these tasty creatures would throw themselves at your feet? It ain't because they like you. They're trying to get a breath of fresh air. A jubilee is a natural phenomenon where a specific series of conditions causes low-oxygen water inside the bay. Most fish can swim above this low oxygen, but the bottom-dwellers, such as flounder and shellfish, are unable to avoid it. As the oxygen-poor water moves toward shore, the bottom-dwellers—which occupy hundreds of acres in Mobile Bay—swim out ahead of it and become trapped on shore. The whole area, sometimes a distance of fifteen miles, teems with the yummy morsels. And, because the lack of oxygen disables them, catching them is as easy as picking up litter on the beach. Mobile Bay is the only body of water where the specific conditions leading to a jubilee occur fairly regularly in the summer. So next time you visit, look for a cloudy day with a gentle east wind, a calm bay surface, and a rising tide. There's just one catch: Jubilees usually happen between

Jubilee! If you're visiting the Mobile Bay area and hear this cry, grab a gig and the largest bucket you can find—heck, grab two—and follow the crowd to the beach. There you'll find an orgy of seafood wallowing right up on shore. Flounder, shrimp, and crab, all right there for the taking. You can fill your buckets with enough fresh seafood to hold your own festival!

midnight and dawn, but a little loss of sleep is a small price to pay—both for the seafood and the fun!

MARDI GRAS • MOBILE

The real Mardi Gras is in Mobile. The very first Mardi Gras celebration ever was observed by French soldiers in that city in 1703 after having survived a bout of yellow fever. To celebrate, they painted their faces red and danced and went crazy for a while. Going crazy for a while is a good thing, so they made the celebration an annual event.

The event really began to take off in 1830, when a group of friends got tipsy at a restaurant. After their meal, the rowdy revelers commandeered some farm implements on display at a local hardware store. Cow bells, rakes, and hoes in hand, they staged an impromptu parade through the streets of Mobile. Calling themselves the Cowbellion de Rakin Society, they formed the first parading mystic society. Floats were added in 1840, but the Civil War postponed the festivities for a few years. However, it was revived in 1866 when another group of rowdies "borrowed" a coal wagon from a local business and rode through town dressed in costumes. Things just got crazier after that.

Today's celebration is a two-week-long party, building toward a crescendo of revelry on Fat Tuesday—the last day of Mardi Gras. During this time of madness, there are parties in the streets, balls, coronations, and parades, lots and lots of parades—twenty-two of 'em, to be exact. Laissez les bon temps roullex—let the good times roll—is the battle cry. Partiers don strange (but true!) costumes and battle each other for the gaudy strands of beads thrown from parade floats.

During the two-week period, there's at least one parade a day, and on the Saturday, Sunday, and Monday before Fat Tuesday, the number increases to two or three per day. On Fat Tuesday, the wildness reaches its peak, with six parades turning the town inside out. And just as suddenly as it began, the revelry ends. At midnight on Fat Tuesday, Mardi Gras ends. The floats are put away. The costumes are hung in the closet. Rowdy revelers once again become upstanding residents, and peace is restored to Mobile. Until next year.

Poke Salat Festival • Arab

Poke salat is a well-known staple in Alabama and is especially popular among Appalachian mountain folk. For the uninitiated, pokeweed grows profusely in cow pastures. It is a nutritious green that, ironically, is poisonous unless boiled in water correctly. When cooked in a pot all day with a little bacon grease, it tastes a lot like collards, another Alabama favorite. We always assumed that salat was a Southern pronunciation for "salad," though we've recently learned that it's also the German word for "salad."

Anyway, since the 1980s, the good folks of Arab have celebrated the poke salat with a festival that features music, arts and crafts, and plenty of food, including, of course, pots and pots of poke salat. Held in May.

Rattlesnake Rodeo • Covington County

Yep, that's what we said. A Rattlesnake Rodeo. Since 1959,

the good folks of Covington County have been coaxing the toothsome creatures from their dark holes and herding them down the streets of the town in an annual roundup. Held the first weekend in March, the rodeo is kicked off with the crowning of a Rattlesnake Queen. Next comes the rattlesnake races—right down the middle of the street! Then there are snake shows and prizes for the longest, the heaviest, and the fattest snake found. There's also music, arts and crafts, and lots of food. The main menu feature? Rattlesnake, of course, prepared in every way imaginable. And, yes, in case you're wondering, it tastes like chicken.

SOPPIN' DAY FESTIVAL • LOACHAPOKA

Notice how many of these festivals celebrate food? Well, here's another. The Soppin' Day Festival in Loachapoka toasts the making of sorghum. Whoa, Nellie! Pass me them biscuits!

STRAWBERRY FESTIVAL • LOXLEY

One fruity festival is the Strawberry Festival in Loxley, held the second week in April, the peak harvest time in Baldwin County for this tart little berry. There's a carnival, a car show, live music,

The Little Miss Strawberry Pageant is part of the Baldwin County Strawberry Festival in Loxley. Held the second week of April, all proceeds go to the Association of Retarded Citizens of Baldwin Country and the Loxley Elementary School.
Courtesy of the Central Baldwin Chamber of Commerce

arts and crafts, food, and fun. Proceeds from the festival go to the Association of Retarded Citizens of Baldwin County and the Loxley Elementary School.

TRAIL OF TEARS MOTORCYCLE RIDE • WATERLOO

The ride was conceived by Jerry Davis, a Scottsboro Harley rider, as a way to commemorate the pain suffered by Native Americans during their forcible removal to reservations in Oklahoma in 1838. More than 17,000 Cherokee men, women, and children were driven from their homes and forced to walk the 1,000 miles to Oklahoma. An estimated 4,000 people died on the way, and many more suffered hunger and sickness. The route taken on that dark walk through history has long been called the Trail of Tears.

The motorcycle ride follows the portion of the Trail of Tears that passes from Chattanooga, Tennessee, to Waterloo, Alabama. The first ride in 1994 began with eight motorcycles and ended with one hundred. There's nothing bikers like more than an excuse to ride, and word quickly spread, spurring phenomenal growth. In 2004, more than 100,000 bikes participated, making it the world's largest organized motorcycle ride—and an awesome sight.

WATERMELON FESTIVAL • RUSSELLVILLE

No doubt about it, there's nuttin' better than ice-cold, sweet watermelon on a hot summer day. Little wonder, then, that there's an award-winning event celebrating this sticky fruit. The Southeast Tourism Society has named Russellville's Watermelon

Funny Happenin's Here

Festival a Top 20 Event, and with good reason. There's a 35- and a 65-mile bike ride, a 5K and a 1K walk, live music, rides, antique cars and trucks, arts and crafts, and lots and lots of free watermelon. Oh, and don't miss out on the watermelon contests, such as the best decorated, the largest, best tasting, and the most unusual. By far, the favorite contest with the kids is the seed-spitting contest. Where else can you spit in public and have your mama cheer you on rather than smack your bottom? The festival is held during the dog days of August, right when the watermelon is at its sweetest and most appreciated!

WORLD CHAMPIONSHIP DOMINO TOURNAMENT • ANDALUSIA

At the other end of the spectrum from Mardi Gras is the World Championship Domino Tournament held in Andalusia. No wild partying here. Just family-oriented domino competitions. Don't scoff. Dominoes have been played by kings and presidents, and even one pharaoh that we know of. The oldest known domino set was found in the tomb of Tutankhamen, pharaoh of Egypt in BC 1355. They haven't been playing dominoes quite that long in Andalusia, but 2004 did mark the twenty-eighth year for the World Championship here. Hey, and there's money involved! More than $450,000 has been awarded since the inception of the tournament in 1976. Folks come from all over the country to play in the tournament, which, of course, concludes Saturday evening. For, if you'll remember, it's against the law to play dominoes on Sunday.

WORLD'S LONGEST YARD SALE • GADSDEN

That's 450 miles of someone else's junk on sale. Kicking off in Gadsden, the sale travels up U.S. Highway 127 to Chattanooga, then continues on Lookout Mountain Parkway through Tennessee and all the way to Covington, Kentucky. With more than 1,000 yard sale vendors in Alabama alone, you'd swear Vulcan's garage exploded and landed on Lookout Mountain. There's a treasure trove of antiques, collectibles, furniture, homemade jams, dishes, and farm machinery. Need a lava lamp? How 'bout a stuffed moose? Maybe a horse-drawn hearse? No home should be without one! There is also lots of food and live entertainment. The four-day event begins the fourth Thursday in August.

Beginning the fourth Thursday in August, the World's Largest Yard Sale runs 450 miles, from Gadsden to Covington, Kentucky. With a host of food, live entertainment, and more than 1,000 vendors in Alabama alone, there is plenty to do at this four-day event.

Pastimes: Past and Present

Alabamians spend their leisure time in lots of ways and in lots of places. Here are some they enjoy.

ALABAMA THEATRE • BIRMINGHAM

Also known as the Showplace of the South, this is one of the most elegant theaters in the country. It has been a popular attraction since it opened to the media on Christmas Day, 1927, and to the public the following day at noon.

The atmosphere alone would be worth the trip here, with what has been called "Spanish/Moorish" architecture, done in rich colors of red, green, and gold. Ambiance is enhanced by the thousands of light bulbs of red, blue, amber, and white. But the highlight of any visit is the Mighty Wurlitzer pipe organ, nicknamed "Big Bertha." It is raised or lowered as needed for any occasion. This is one of the few Wurlitzer pipe organs still in its original installation.

The Alabama Theatre, "Showplace of the South," features elegant decor and the Mighty Wurlitzer, "Big Bertha." Courtesy of the Alabama Theatre

Pastimes: Past and Present

Even with all its majesty, the Alabama Theatre is not just a shrine to a time gone by. Events are still held here, and movies are still shown. Of particular note is the holiday film series, which includes *It's A Wonderful Life, White Christmas,* as well as animated favorites like *Frosty the Snowman* and *Rudolph the Red Nosed Reindeer.* The theatre's five stories and 2,200 seats distributed among a main level, mezzanine, and balcony offer views sure to please anyone.

Check for scheduled events by calling the theatre or going to its web site, and see a classic at this classic located in downtown Birmingham at 1817 3rd Avenue North.

Birmingham International Raceway (BIR) • Birmingham

BIR, as the racetrack is commonly called, is a 5/8 mile paved oval located at the Alabama State Fairgrounds near Birmingham. But it didn't start out that way.

It was originally built as a dirt track for horse racing in 1889 by the Birmingham Jockey Club. It was used as the State Fair Grounds until 1900 when the State Fair was moved to Montgomery. In 1925, the track welcomed auto racing and hosted a huge automobile extravaganza and has never looked back since.

The facility was used by stock and sprint car promoters throughout the '50s and '60s. Finally in 1962, new owners set the goal of making it a premier facility with an overhaul that included paving the 73-year-old track, thus ending dirt racing in Birmingham. BIR then started to host the NASCAR Grand National and Winston Cup events. Lights were added in 1966 and two years later, the track was resurfaced to "Talladega specifications," complete with caution lights.

Located one mile off exit 120 on Interstate 59/20, 2331 Bessemer Road in Birmingham.

ETERNAL WORD TELEVISION NETWORK • IRONDALE

What do a nun and a television station have in common? No, it's not a riddle, there really is such a combination in our own state, and it's at the Eternal Word Television Network in Irondale. But just how did that unlikely pairing come about?

In the early 1960s, Mother M. Angelica, a Poor Clare nun, cloistered and dedicated to the perpetual Adoration of the Most Blessed Sacrament, founded Our Lady of Angels Monastery in Irondale. She began to write "mini-books," which contained short teachings on a variety of religious topics. As their popularity grew, the nuns obtained a printing press, and started distributing the books worldwide.

> At 81 years of age, Mother Angelica was honored at the Alabama Broadcasters Association's 2004 Annual Convention as the organization's "Citizen of the Year."

Soon, Mother Angelica began receiving requests for speaking engagements, which evolved into a video series of her talks. As demand for the videos grew, Mother Angelica, who knew little of the world of technology and communication, built her own TV studio in a garage on monastery property. The facility has evolved into a state-of-the-art audiovisual complex known as Eternal Word Television Network, which airs family and religious programming from a Catholic point of view in English and Spanish. More than 80 percent of its programming is original. The work is funded entirely by gifts, and the station is visited by thousands of pilgrims annually.

Visitors of all faiths are welcomed to be part of the audience of EWTN shows or to attend a televised Mass or spiritual talk. Tickets for tapings are free, but due to limited seating, reservations are required. Check the web site at www.ewtn.com for availability and information on upcoming guests.

The studio is located at 5817 Old Leeds Road in Irondale.

FOOTBALL IN THE GREAT STATE OF ALABAMA

Roll Tide! War Eagle! Football in Alabama is not just a game; it's a hallowed tradition. And that's college ball, son. None of those high-paid professionals for us. Regardless of whether you are a football fan, to live in this state, you must declare an allegiance to one of the state's two biggest teams—the Alabama Crimson Tide or the Auburn Tigers. Here's a few little-known facts about these two great teams.

- The Crimson Tide is the only team in the nation to win more than once at the four biggest bowl games: the Sugar Bowl, the Rose Bowl, the Orange Bowl, and the Cotton Bowl.

Legend has it that Alabama's renowned coach Paul "Bear" Bryant earned his nickname as a teenager in Arkansas by wrestling a bear at a carnival. Must have been one of those "Hey, Bubba, watch this!" moments.

- Auburn has produced two Heisman Trophy winners: Pat Sullivan in 1971 and Bo Jackson in 1985.

- The University of Alabama is one of the nation's most winning college football teams. In its first 100 years, the team had an extraordinary record: 682-234-43.

- During the 1980s Auburn won or shared four SEC Championships and was consistently listed in the Top 10 national poll rankings.

- Eight Auburn players have been inducted into the College Football Hall of Fame: Terry Beasley, Tucker Frederickson, Walter Gilbert, Jimmy Hitchcock, Bo Jackson, Ralph "Shug" Jordan, Tracy Rocker, and Pat Sullivan.

- In 1926, Alabama became the first Southern team ever to play in the Rose Bowl. After squeaking by Washington 20-19, they also became the first Southern team to win the Rose Bowl. Roll Tide!

- Auburn's 1994 victory over LSU featured one of the most bizarre finishes ever witnessed in football. With LSU winning 23-9 going into the fourth quarter, Auburn safety Ken Alvis picked off an LSU pass and ran 42 yards for a touchdown. Next Fred Smith picked off another LSU pass and scored on a 32-yard run, followed quickly by another pickoff by Brian Robinson for a 41-yard run. Before the quarter was over, Auburn had intercepted five passes and beat LSU 30-26, keeping alive a 14-game winning streak.

Toomer's Corner, at the intersection of College Street and Magnolia Avenue in Auburn, is a popular gathering place for students of Auburn University. Their activities include "rolling" the trees with toilet tissue after any football win, home or away. "Rolling Toomer's" has become one of Auburn's greatest traditions since it was started in the early 1960s.

- The longest touchdown pass play in Alabama history was a 94-yard Hail Mary from quarterback Freddie Kitchens to Michael Vaughn in the 1996 SEC Championship game against Florida.

- Nineteen Alabama players/coaches have been inducted into the College Football Hall of Fame: Johnny Mac Brown, Paul "Bear" Bryant, Johnny Cain, Harry Gilmer, John Hannah, Frank Howard, Dixie Howell, Pooley Hubert, Don Hutson, Lee Roy Jordan, Vaughn Mancha, Johnny Musso, Billy

Neighbors, Ozzie Newsome, Fred Sington, Riley Smith, Frank Thomas, Wallace Wade, and Don Whitmire.

- Alabama has won twelve national championships, six of them when coached by the Bear.

- Auburn's first game was played in Atlanta on February 20, 1892, where Auburn defeated Georgia 10-0 and kicked off one of the oldest rivalries in the South.

- Alabama holds the record for Sugar Bowl wins. The Crimson Tide has won eight, with three of those consecutive wins in 1978, 1979, and 1980. Ah, the good old days!

- The Tiger Walk is a tradition that began in the early 1960s when Auburn players walked from Sewell Hall to the stadium. Fans would line Donahue Drive to wish them well. According to legend, the largest Tiger Walk occurred before the 1989 Alabama/Auburn game when more than 20,000 screaming fans lined the street. The Tiger Walk occurs two hours before the game.

The first Alabama/Auburn game was played in Birmingham in 1893 and was won by Auburn 32-22. Auburn, in fact, dominated the Iron Bowl, as it became known, in the first years, winning seven of eleven games.

Pastimes: Past and Present

- Alabama became known as the Crimson Tide in 1907 when Hugh Roberts, sports editor of the *Birmingham Age-Herald*, compared the football players to a red tide as he watched them play Auburn in a "sea" of red mud. Zipp Newman, sports editor for *The Birmingham News*, made the moniker more popular when, in 1919, he wrote that the team reminded him of a powerful ocean of red (the color of the team's jerseys) repeatedly pounding the shore.

- Auburn's first bowl trip was the Bacardi Bowl played in Havana, Cuba on New Year's Day in 1937. Auburn and Villanova tied 7-7.

- In 1995, Coach Paul "Bear" Bryant was named in the *Guinness Book of World Records* as coach with the most wins ever. The Bear's 323-85-17 record held until 2001, when Penn State's Joe Paterno put away his 324th win (though Paterno subsequently lost the record only two years later).

For reasons not fully known, the Iron Bowl was suspended from 1907 until 1948, when it resumed and was played for the first time at Birmingham's Legion Field, a neutral ground for both teams. This venue became tradition for the game between the two rivals. Alabama stomped Auburn 55-0 that first year, lost the next year, but won the next four. Then the pendulum swung back to Auburn, who had a five-year winning streak going when Alabama hired legendary coach Paul "Bear" Bryant.

The Bear began an unprecedented domination of the game in the 1960s. As the rivalry between the two schools intensified, television developed an interest in the game. The Iron Bowl was televised for the first time on November 26, 1964. Alabama was enjoying an undefeated season. Auburn's season was a bit less lustrous, 6-3, but they were coming to the game after consecutive wins over Mississippi State and Georgia, two of the toughest teams in the SEC. They also had the advantage of having upset the Tide in the previous year's Iron Bowl.

For the first time ever, a national television audience got a glimpse at the backyard brawl that is Alabama football. In an all-out war, the two teams battled up and down the field. Auburn's All-America fullback, Tucker Frederickson ran all over Alabama's defense, but in the end, that didn't matter one whit. Auburn just could not contain Alabama's star quarterback, a young guy named Joe Willie Namath. In a hard-fought game, the Tide won 21-14.

Bryant continued his domination of the game—and college football—until his retirement in 1982, the ending of an era. There was another ending of an era in 1989, when Auburn finally won the right to have its home games played in Auburn. Alabama continued to have its games played at Legion Field

Jacksonville State University student Ashley Martin became the first woman to play and score in a Division I football game, kicking three extra points in three tries for her school against Cumberland in an August 30, 2001 game. She helped her team defeat Cumberland 72-10.

until 2000, when the Iron Bowl was played for the first time in Alabama's Tuscaloosa stadium.

Throughout that time, through numerous coaching changes on both sides, the balance of power has swung between the two teams, but the intense rivalry has never abated. As of 2004, with Auburn winning three consecutive Iron Bowls, Alabama still holds a slight edge in the record: 38-30-1.

FLOATING CONDOMINIUMS • GUNTERSVILLE

People often say they have "a place *on* the river" when what they really mean is "a place *near* the river." But at Lake Guntersville, you really can have a place on the river if you own or rent one of the new floating condominiums at Spring Lake Marina. There they sit, all in a row, locked together and moored in the marina.

Condos have the look of the rustic hunting cabins that inspired them. They were modified to float atop rubber-coated Styrofoam billets. Each one offers ample room in the 36 x 12 cabin and surprising luxury. The bedroom features a queen-sized bed, bath, and full-sized shower. The mini kitchen is fully equipped, and the benches at the kitchen table even turn into a bed. In all, the condos can sleep five. If that's not enough, there's a fireplace and a TV with 100-channel satellite connections. And those aren't the only conveniences available: There are eleven restaurants within walking distance. Or you can always step outside and catch your dinner without ever stepping off your front porch.

Located on Highway 431 in Guntersville.

GYMNO-VITA PARK • VANDIVER

If you're interested in visiting somewhere really unusual, how about a nudist colony? And better yet, what about one that's "family friendly"? That's what the ad says for Gymno-Vita Park in Vandiver. In fact, only families and couples are allowed, no singles.

A wealth of activities is offered: swimming, camping, hiking, ping-pong, table games, and pool are just a few of your options. If you like dancing, there's the Pink Champagne Ballroom and Theater. Just for children, there's a playroom called the "Monkey Cage." Anyone interested in just passing the time of day will appreciate the new lodge, which offers more than 5,000 square feet of space for meeting and greeting other visitors, with 1,000 square feet of porches with rocking chairs and a porch swing (no splinters, please!).

Don't think about contacting them by e-mail, fax, or 800 number: They don't have any of those. You'll have to use the good ol' U.S. Mail or the telephone, but do be sure to call ahead.

RICKWOOD FIELD • BIRMINGHAM

Step through the gates of Rickwood Field and you travel back into baseball's glory years. Everywhere you look are remnants from another time: the antique light towers erected in 1936, when Rickwood became one of the first minor league parks to host nighttime baseball; the gazebo-style press box, an exact replica of the original 1910 structure; the drop-in scoreboard recreated to its 1948 specifications; all this, punctuated by vintage signs and, occasionally, period uniforms.

Modeled after Forbes Field in Pittsburgh, this working

tribute to a bygone era was the brainchild of Alabama industrialist Rick Woodward. While still in his 20s, Woodward bought controlling interest in the city's professional baseball team, the Coal Barons. He sought and received help from the legendary Connie Mark to design "The Finest Minor League Ballpark Ever" in a town that was then the fastest growing city in the nation. Woodward's idea not only caught on, but received such support that on opening day, August 18, 1910, the entire city closed in honor of the event. The Barons played

Rickwood Field boasts to be America's oldest ballpark. Such legends as Babe Ruth, Shoeless Joe Jackson, and Willie Mays have played on its turf.
Courtesy of Graham Knight
www.BaseballPilgrimages.com

there until 1987, when they moved into the suburban Hoover Metropolitan Stadium. Since 1996 they have returned for one afternoon game per year, making Rickwood the oldest professional ballpark still in use today.

In its heyday, this facility hosted some of the greatest players in history before standing-room-only crowds. It saw the likes of Babe Ruth, Roger Hornsby, and "Shoeless" Joe Jackson, not to mention a brash, young Dizzy Dean bested by Ray Caldwell in the twilight of his career. The newly formed Black

Barons of the Negro American League, which gave a 16-year-old Willie Mays his start as a center-fielder, alternated weekends with the Barons. They provided an unforgettable experience for those who came to watch Negro League standouts such as all-time Negro American League home run record holder George "Mule" Suttles.

And this diamond continues to shine. It served as the backdrop to such movies as *Cobb* (1994) and *Soul of the Game* (1995). It still sees occasional play by various leagues and is open daily for free, self-guided tours through the stands, into the dugouts, onto the field, and behind the outfield fence. Few historical places offer such access.

The park is located at 1137 2nd Avenue West in Birmingham. Come for a visit and see the game America fell in love with long ago.

.

Strange But True Culture

Artistes, world-class storytellers, music, and music men—it's culture with a twist in Strange But True Alabama.

Artists

Hard times affect people differently. For some, the hard times become a hammer that beats them down. Others take that hammer and beat the hard times into art that touches the world.

LONNIE HOLLEY

Birmingham native Lonnie Holley is one of those hard-time artists. He was only four years old when he was taken from his mother and later sold to a bootlegger for a pint of whiskey. Years of abuse followed, as he was shuffled to foster homes around the Southeast. At age fourteen, after a short stint in a juvenile detention center, his grandmother brought him back to Birmingham to live in the

Birmingham native Lonnie Holley has been nationally recognized for his yard art, which he creates out of discarded sandstone and Elmer's glue. Today, he and his artwork reside in Harpersville.
Courtesy of Catherine Crenshaw

family's small house next to the Birmingham International Airport. Times were still hard, but at least he had a family.

When his sister's two children were killed in a house fire in 1979, the family was too poor to afford gravestones. Despondent over the death of his niece and nephew, Holley contemplated suicide, but instead he picked up a hammer and beat back the hard times. Using what he had at hand— discarded sandstone, a by-product of a local steel mill, and kitchen utensils as tools—he carved headstones for the tiny graves. Inspired by what he had done, he began covering the quarter-acre yard with his artwork, all made from salvaged material. He worked in sandstone, wire, and wood, taking trash and turning it into meaningful art.

Word of Holley's yard art gallery spread, and after his "discovery" by the director of the Birmingham Museum of Art, his work began appearing in big city shows and galleries around the country. His work has been exhibited at the White House and in 1981 was included in the Smithsonian exhibition "More Land Than Sky: Art From Appalachia."

Despite his growing fame as a folk artist and the hefty sums he began to command for his art, Holley planned to remain at his family home, where he was surrounded by his art. The Birmingham International Airport had other ideas, however. Holley's homestead was in the middle of a planned expansion, and the airport authority wanted him out. He was offered only what the land was worth, without consideration for the value of his yard gallery and the difficulty involved in moving the now-expensive artwork. When he refused their offer, the airport authority tried to force him out, but they didn't count on that hard-time hammer of his. He took them to court and won a settlement large enough to move both his family and his artwork to fifteen acres in Shelby County's Harpersville.

Although he could now easily afford conventional art supplies, Holley continued to use found materials to create his art. For his sandstone carvings, he still used discarded core sand, the inner core lining of sand used in steel making. To seal his finished works, he applied a coat of plain old Elmer's glue.

CHARLIE LUCAS

Folk artists. Self-taught artists. Outsiders. Whatever you call them, it's been said that there's just one rule in folk art: The artist must be as interesting as his art. That's certainly true of Charlie Lucas, known in the art world as "Tin Man." Despite the fact that he was unable to read or write, Lucas has gained international fame for his artwork and even spent two months as an artist-in-residence in France.

Another hard-time artist, Lucas began working in metal sculptures after a back injury put him off work for more than a year. With just $10 in his pocket and a family to feed, Lucas turned to God for help and received the inspiration to use scrap metal to make art.

As a child he had wanted to be an artist and had spent many hours making his own toys. When he expressed an interest in studying art in school, his teachers told him he had to learn a trade. "Art is for white people," they told him.

But now, God was telling him to fulfill that dream. He

gathered scrap metal from local junkyards and welded them into intricate sculptures—his toys, he calls them—which he placed in his Prattville yard. He filled his sculpture garden with gigantic birds, dinosaurs, airplanes, tin men, and a myriad of other items. In using scrap metal, he has said he is showing that, like his life, "You can take the scrap from the bottom of the heap and breathe new life into it."

JIMMIE LEE SUDDUTH

Now here's an example of good old Alabama ingenuity: Fayette's Jimmie Lee Sudduth painted with mud. Mud mixed with sugar to make it stick. He also used coffee grounds, tobacco, and plants, such as turnip greens, watermelon vines, and berries, to add color. He discovered this technique as a child while on a walk in the woods. He mixed mud with honey and painted a face on a tree stump and was amazed to find it still there days later.

That was in 1913, when Sudduth was just three years old. He began painting then, mixing the mud he found around his rural home with sugar and painting it on plywood scraps. As he grew, he spent much time perfecting his technique and said he could identify thirty-six different shades of mud around his Fayette home, though he began to use house paint for color, as well. His work was discovered in 1970, and since that time, he has gained international fame as a folk artist.

Sudduth's subjects have expanded somewhat because of the experience of his fame. Several pictures depicting New York skyscrapers can be found among the paintings of Southern mansions, rural homes, and down-home people. Visitors to Sudduth's home often found themselves entertained by his wit, painting demonstrations, and sometimes a harmonica serenade.

MOSE TOLLIVER

Mose Tolliver began painting in the late 1960s, after an accident left him crippled and depressed. He would hang his crude paintings on the trees around his Montgomery home, asking just a dollar or two if a passerby showed interest. Word got around, as word does, and eventually Tolliver's plywood paintings came to the attention of the art world. In 1982, his work was featured in the exhibition of Black Folk Art in America at the Corcoran Gallery in Washington, D.C. The show introduced Tolliver as a major self-taught artist.

Artist Mose Tolliver has been featured in the Black Folk Art in America exhibition at the Corcoran Gallery in Washington, D.C. His works depict abstract views of plants, animals, and people using plywood and house paint.
Courtesy of Keith Boyer

Tolliver continued working out of his home on Sayre Street in Montgomery, right next to the house that Zelda Fitzgerald grew up in, even after his popularity—and wealth—grew. Artwork no longer hung from the trees, but he still sat on the end of his bed to paint, using the materials at hand—plywood and house paint.

His work depicts abstract views of plants, animals, and people, especially women. Many paintings are of an erotic nature, a fact that often irked his wife, Willie Mae, who died in 1991.

The art world calls his color schemes harmonious and sophisticated. Tolliver might say that's the colors he had on hand at the time. They also find him inventive for his use of improvised hangers—discarded aluminum can rings. A 1981 quote in the *Montgomery Advertiser* may well sum up his feelings. "I'm not interested in art," he said. "I just want to paint my pictures."

Inventors

Alabama is full of inventive people. Here are just a few of them and their creations and discoveries.

MARY ANDERSON

Little is known about this inventor, except in connection with her famous invention, the windshield wiper. During a trip to New York in 1903, Anderson noticed that if it was raining, streetcar drivers had to open car windows to see or stop their cars, get out, and remove snow and ice. She figured there had to be a better way to do this, so she invented a swinging arm device with a rubber blade, operated by the driver with a lever.

When she applied for a patent, Henry Ford's Model A had not even been manufactured yet, and he wouldn't create his famed Model T until 1908. Anderson was teased about her creation by people who thought the wipers would be more of a distraction than a help. But those people stopped laughing when the windshield wiper became standard equipment on all cars by 1916.

GEORGE WASHINGTON CARVER

Who would have thought you could get as much out of a simple peanut as George Washington Carver did? But that's not all. Besides the 325 products he created from peanuts, Carver also developed 108 from sweet potatoes, and seventy-five from pecans. Among the products developed or improved are such everyday items as axle grease, bleach, buttermilk, chili sauce, metal polish, meat tenderizer, shoe polish, and shaving cream.

Carver spent much of his life in Tuskegee, where he had moved at the request of Booker T. Washington to accept a position as instructor at the Tuskegee Normal and Industrial Institute. His work in developing industrial applications from agricultural products derived 118 products, including a rubber substitute and more than 500 dyes and pigments, from twenty-eight different plants. He was responsible for the invention of a process for producing paints and stains from soybeans, for which three separate patents were issued.

Carver worked at a time when the South had been dependent on cotton and tobacco, which had depleted the soil. Carver's newly developed method of crop rotation encouraged the planting of soil-enriching crops such as peanuts, soybeans, and sweet potatoes, virtually revolutionizing southern agriculture. Not only did he offer more crops to plant, but more ways to use the products from the crops that grew.

Carver did not patent or profit from most of his products, giving his discoveries freely to mankind. He felt that he could not sell his ideas, since they were gifts from God to begin with. The epitaph on his grave, next to that of Booker T.

Washington's in Tuskeegee, appropriately reads, "He could have added fortune to fame, but caring for neither, he found happiness and honor in being helpful to the world."

BOB GALLAGHER

If you have ever placed a call for help, or if you ever have to, you can thank Bob Gallagher for making this possible. Most people won't recognize Bob's name, but he is responsible for initiating and directing the effort to get 911 service in our country. You see, while people in Great Britain could call 999 for help as early as 1937, the United States didn't have this service. But Congress began to talk about having this in our country as well, and by 1967, had legally mandated that it be developed.

The story goes that the Federal Trade Commission, along with AT&T, announced plans to establish the service first in Indiana. Bob Gallagher, President of Alabama Telephone, was annoyed that he hadn't been contacted about the plans. So he decided to beat AT&T to the punch. After getting all the proper approvals, Gallagher and his team worked nonstop to get the system up and running. The work was completed on February 16, 1968, at exactly 2:00 p.m. At that time, the workers reportedly celebrated with a team cheer of "Bingo!"

The first American 911 call was made on February 16, 1966 in Haleyville, AL. The call was made by Alabama Speaker of the House Rankin Fite and answered by State Representative Tom Bevill.

Dr. James D. Hardy

Dr. James Hardy, an Alabama native, performed the world's first human lung transplant at the University Hospital in Jackson, Mississippi, on June 11, 1963. An interesting historical note is that during that surgery, Dr. Hardy was to have been assisted by one of his residents, Dr. Martin Dalton, but Dr. Dalton was called to the emergency room to see a gunshot patient. That patient was Medgar Evers, the civil rights worker who had been shot at his home.

Not content with one "first," Dr. Hardy and his team performed the first heart transplant into a human just a few months later, on January 23, 1964. Hardy at first drew criticism because the heart he transplanted was from a chimpanzee, not a human. But the science community later recognized the significant contribution for what it was, and Dr. Hardy received the honors he deserved.

Dr. Percy Julian

This Montgomery native and world-renowned chemist is best known for producing chemicals in a lab that were previously found only in nature. He discovered a synthetic cortisone substitute, radically less expensive but just as effective as cortisone. Whereas natural cortisone had to be extracted from the adrenal glands of oxen at a significant cost, Julian's synthetic version was only pennies per ounce. He was also responsible for developing synthetic versions of hormones that we're very familiar with today, progesterone and testosterone.

Quite by accident, while working as lab director at Glidden

Company, Julian also invented Aerofoam, a compound used to put out gasoline and oil fires. He was inducted into the Inventors Hall of Fame in 1990.

WALDO L. SEMON

Another Hall of Fame inductee is Waldo Semon of Demopolis. who turned polyvinyl chloride (PVC), into vinyl. Although PVC had been invented by a German chemist in 1872, Semon turned it into a useful material that became the world's second-best selling plastic.

Music From the Heart

Hank Williams Sr. Hank Williams Jr. Percy Sledge. Alabama. Jimmy Buffett. Tammy Wynette. Lionel Richie and The Commodores. The Temptations. Emmylou Harris. Wilson Pickett. Alabama has been rocking the world for decades. But these folks and their music are well known and nowhere near as interesting as our Strange But True Alabama music and the people who make it.

ALABAMA JAZZ HALL OF FAME

This tribute to legendary musicians is housed in the restored Carver Theater, which was opened as the Carver Performing Arts Center. The museum honors great jazz artists with ties to the state of Alabama, such as Nat King Cole, Duke Ellington, Amos Gordon, Lionel Hampton, and Erskine Hawkins, a local music educator who wrote Glenn Miller's hit, "Tuxedo Junction." The museum features costumes, musical instruments, records, and playbills of various artists, recalling the glory days of jazz.

The museum is located in the Civil Rights District at 1631 4th Avenue North.

Alabama was honored in a unique way when Ft. Payne cousins Randy Owen, Teddy Gentry, and Jeff Cook got together to play country music. They originally played under the names "Young Country" and "Wildcountry." But they found their place in country music when they added Mark Herndon to the mix and renamed the group "Alabama" in honor of their state. They became the first group ever to be named the Country Music Association's Entertainer of the year and was the Academy of Country Music's Artist of the Decade for the '80s.

FIVE BLIND BOYS OF ALABAMA

Gospel music, too, has a rich history in Alabama. In fact, one of gospel music's longest-lived acts is from Alabama. The Five Blind Boys of Alabama came together in 1937 at the Alabama Institute for the Deaf and Blind in Talladega, where all were students. Except for one brief breakup, they've been together ever since.

As students of the institution, the boys were being taught menial skills, such as broom making, which at that time, was believed to be one of the few viable skills open to the blind. They knew they'd never make a decent living with those skills, but while in the Institute's choir, they discovered their salvation.

The group—Clarence Fountain, Jimmy Carter, George Scott, Johnny Fields, Vel Bozman Traylor, and Ollice Thomas—admired gospel groups, such as the Golden Gate Quartet and the Soul Stirrers, who had become popular and were making good money traveling the country. The boys formed a group they called the Happy Land Jubilee Singers and polished their act at the Institute. They hit the road in 1945 and never looked back.

The first five years they spent touring the Southeast, living a hand-to-mouth existence and staying mainly around Birmingham. In 1947 Vel Traylor died, leaving five members. It wasn't until 1949, when their record *I Can See Everybody's Mother But Mine* hit the charts, that the group finally became known.

The name change came about when a promoter from New Jersey decided to pit another group, the Five Blind Boys of Mississippi, in a contest against the group. They changed their name and toured with the Mississippi group for many years, often going head to head in a great singing rivalry.

After lean times through the 1970s and 1980s, gospel music is experiencing a revival, and the Blind Boys of Alabama are going stronger than ever, though they have added a few new members. They have sung at the White House and the U.S. Olympic Games, appeared on Broadway with Morgan Freeman, and have recorded songs with such artists as Bonnie Raitt, K.D. Lang, and Peter Gabriel. Their CD *Spirit of the Century* won the 2002 Grammy award for the Best Traditional Soul Gospel Album. From broom-making to singing in the White House, not a bad bit of sweeping up for five blind boys from Alabama.

SACRED HARP MUSIC

Although Sacred Harp music's origins lie in colonial New England, Alabama is now the acknowledged cultural center for this centuries-old musical form. Every summer, enthusiasts from all over the world travel to Birmingham to attend the National Sacred Harp Music Convention, and Alabamians have been instrumental in keeping the music alive.

If you've never heard of Sacred Harp music, the first thing you should know is that there's no harp. In fact, the only instruments used in Sacred Harp music are the singers' voices, and they are LOUD, so loud that the music is sometimes called loud hymns. It's also called fasola music for the notes sung, or shape-note music because of the unique shape of the printed notes.

One particular hotbed of Sacred Harp music is Liberty Baptist Church in Henagar. This church has a long tradition in the music and has helped to keep Sacred Harp music alive for 110 years. The singers of Liberty Baptist gained national recognition for their participation in the critically acclaimed movie *Cold Mountain*, which featured two songs by the group. Stars Nicole Kidman and Jude Law were taught the music, and their voices were added to the soundtrack.

Traditionally rooted in the white culture, Sacred Harp music has enjoyed a rich African-American tradition in southeast Alabama, thanks mainly to Bryhill native Judge Jackson. Jackson began Sacred Harp singing as a teenager and was composing his own songs by age twenty-one. In 1927, he submitted several of these compositions to the all-white committee charged with revising *The Sacred Harp* (1844), the hymn book that established the singing tradition. When all of his compositions were rejected, Jackson compiled his own hymnal containing his original compositions and those of other area African-Americans. *The Colored Sacred Harp*, published in 1934, has become an important historical document in this musical tradition.

Jackson's son, Japheth Jackson, is carrying on his father's tradition. As a leader in the African-American Sacred Harp community, he has been instrumental in bringing national attention to his small Ozark group, the Wiregrass Sacred Harp Singers. The group performed at the Festival of American Folklife at the Smithsonian Institute in 1970 and have performed all over the country. Japheth was awarded the Alabama Folk Heritage Award in 1988.

W.C. Handy

Florence native William Christopher Handy is known as the "Father of the Blues" because he was the first to blend the African-American ballads and spiritual "field hollers" of the Deep South with the style of popular ragtime and jazz. His 1912 hit "Memphis Blues" and the 1914 hit "St. Louis Blues" are heralded as the beginnings of popular blues music.

Florence native W. C. Handy is known as the "Father of the Blues." His 150 songs helped to bring African-American music to mainstream culture. Courtesy of the Florence Department of Art and Museums

Handy acknowledged that he did not invent the blues, a style of music that strongly expressed the bleak realities of the African-American experience of the time. Bad luck, racial strife, trouble, and lost love always figured into blues music. Handy said he merely transcribed the blues and presented them to the world.

Maybe so, but Handy's collection of 150 songs became the standard for both African-American and white jazz artists and served to bring African-American music to the mainstream culture.

The city of Florence maintains the restored log cabin where Handy was born and holds a festival every year in his honor.

Writers

Alabama can proudly claim an abundance of talented writers. Nationally-acclaimed ones, too, like Harper Lee, who still lives quietly in our own Monroeville. But there are some whose personalities or the topics that brought them notoriety are just plain strange. Here are a few you may recognize.

TRUMAN CAPOTE

Lots of words describe this writer: eccentric, unusual, controversial, flamboyant, strange. Oh, and one more: Alabamian.

Truman Capote (whose birth name was Truman Streckfus Persons) wasn't born in Alabama, but he was transplanted here to live with an aunt in Monroeville when his parents divorced. He spent most of his childhood here, and the imprint of Monroe County would later be seen in such works as *A Christmas Memory, The Grass Harp,* and *Other Voices.* When his mother remarried, Truman went to live with her in New York, taking his stepfather's surname.

Capote began to write stories when he was only eight years old. He found work at the *New Yorker* when he was seventeen but was later fired for angering Robert Frost at a reading. He plugged along in his attempts to write and published his first story, "Miriam," winning an O. Henry award for short stories. By 1947, *Life* had profiled him as one of the country's up-and-coming writers.

The beginning of the 1960s found Capote riding high on the success of his novella *Breakfast at Tiffany's,* but it was his next work that would revolutionize modern literature by creation of a new genre, the non-fiction novel. *In Cold Blood,* universally recognized as his masterpiece, told the story of the senseless murder of the Clutter family on a farm in Garden City, Kansas, reported in the *New York Times* on November 16, 1959. Two men were captured and found guilty of the crime, for which they were executed in 1965. Capote was present at the executions, sort of: he watched the first hanging but ran out of the warehouse where the gallows were located before the second one. Capote researched the story for six years, enmeshing himself in the lives of the killers and the townspeople and taking thousands of pages of notes. His account of the crime was published in part in the *New Yorker* in 1965 and as a book the following year. Capote later said that if he had known the emotional toll the book would take on him, he would never have started it.

With success came celebrity. Capote wanted to be known, and he took pride in knowing "everyone." As a child, he had made friends in Monroeville with Harper Lee, who portrayed him as Dill in her world famous novel, *To Kill A Mockingbird.* As an adult, he loved to tell that he personally knew JFK, RFK, Lee Harvey Oswald, and Sirhan Sirhan, all completely independently of each other, before the tragic assassinations. He was an intimate of Andy Warhol. The two met in 1951, and Warhol said he wrote to Capote every day for a year. Warhol also said that he and Capote were secretly engaged for ten years, exchanging naked photographs instead of rings.

Capote earned the nickname "the tiny terror" for his love for gossip. He began work on a project to be called *Answered Prayers* after Saint Theresa of Avile's saying that answered prayers cause more tears than unanswered ones. The work was based on thinly disguised stories of his personal friends, and not surprisingly, when the first few chapters were published in *Esquire* magazine, he was shunned by many of the people he wrote about. He didn't understand their anger, figuring that they knew he was a writer and would naturally write about people and things he knew. But their negative response sent him into a spiral of drug and alcohol use. His life deteriorated with his health, and finally he learned that he had only six months to live. When asked what his tombstone should read, he said, "An excuse, a phrase I used about almost any commitment: I TRIED TO GET OUT OF IT, BUT I COULDN'T."

If all this doesn't sound strange enough, consider that Capote couldn't even recite the alphabet, at least not correctly or all the way through, even under hypnosis. He could add and even read upside down, but he couldn't subtract. Doctors would probably be able to diagnose and help those things today. But they were part of the mix that made him an unforgettable character, one he summarized as well as anyone could have: "There's never been anybody like me, and after I'm gone, there ain't ever gonna be anybody like me again." Amen to that!

A historic marker identifies the house where Capote lived with his relatives on South Alabama Avenue in Monroeville, and a self-guided walking tour points it out to interested visitors. An exhibit honoring this famous resident is being prepared at the Old Courthouse Museum.

DENNIS COVINGTON

Have you ever been bored in church? You wouldn't be if you attended the church Dennis Covington visited while he was researching his book *Salvation on Sand Mountain*. The work is a nonfiction account of Covington's ventures into the world of a snake-handling church.

Covington's interest in this unusual topic had been piqued when he read of a preacher arrested for attempting to kill his wife by making her put her hands in a box filled with poisonous serpents. He headed off to Scottsboro to cover the trial but soon found himself attending church services where preachers and parishioners alike lift poisonous serpents in the air and mason jars of strychnine to their lips in proof of God's power to protect them.

The result was a widely acclaimed book that won the Rea Prize from the *Boston Book Review* for the best non-fiction book of

1995 and was a National Book Award nominee.

Dennis Covington is currently Professor of Creative Writing at Texas Tech University in Lubbock, Texas.

WILLIAM BRADFORD HUIE

This Hartselle native managed to be in the middle of some of the sensational events of his time.

His first novel, *Mud on the Stars* (1942), dealt with the depression in the Deep South. Following the war, he wrote his best-selling comic novel, *The Revolt of Mamie Stove*, a Honolulu prostitute who amassed a fortune when the island was swamped with servicemen. In 1954, *The Execution of Private Slovik* drew attention to the case of Michigan-born Eddie Slovik, executed by firing squad for the crime of desertion. During World War II, 21,049 American military personnel were convicted of desertion, forty-nine of whom were sentenced to death. But only Pvt. Slovik paid the ultimate price, an act personally ordered by Dwight D. Eisenhower to discourage other potential deserters.

But Huie was primarily known for writing extensively about the campaign for black civil rights, first about the lynching of a black teenager in Mississippi, Emmett Till. Two white men accused of the crime were acquitted, but Huie did not believe the verdict was correct. He felt that the truth would only come out if a journalist uncovered it, so he paid the men $4,000 for their story. Since they could not be tried again for this same crime, they were free to tell the truth.

When Edward Aaron, a 34-year-old African-American from

Barbour County was castrated, Huie's exposure of this Klan initiation ceremony was reported in *Time* magazine. Two of the Klansmen confessed and testified against the other four, who did not believe an all-white, all-male jury would convict them. Graphic evidence was introduced: Women were excused from the courtroom, and the victim partially undressed to stand before the jury with proof of the crime. None of the defendants denied the atrocity. Each was judged guilty and given twenty years. However, with new appointments to the parole board, the four were not even required to serve any time of their sentences before their parole.

Huie continued his "checkbook journalism," reportedly paying James Earl Ray $40,000 for his story of the assassination of Dr. Martin Luther King Jr. Huie concluded that Ray, acting alone, had committed the murder. Huie was denounced by fellow journalists and readers alike who felt that purchased information was suspect. He defended himself by saying, "I don't recommend it. I just don't know any better way."

Other work included an account of the abduction and murder of three young civil rights activists in Philadelphia. Articles about the murders of James Chaney, Andrew Goodman, and Michael Schwerner were published in 1964 as a book, *Three Lives for Mississippi.* Upon publication of his 1967 exposé on the inner workings of the Ku Klux Klan, *The Klansman,* Huie defended himself with a shotgun as the local Klan burned a cross in his yard.

Huie's twenty-one books sold more than 28 million copies.

Seven were made into Hollywood movies. He held the sales records for three of the nation's leading news magazines that included his articles.

William Bradford Huie is honored annually by the William Bradford Huie/Alabama Collection celebration of writers at Snead State Community College in Boaz, where his wife, Martha, served as head of the art department in the 1970s.

KATHRYN TUCKER WINDHAM

Kathryn Tucker Windham tells tales. And she has lots to tell, beginning with her experience as a woman reporter in the South. In 1939, after graduating from Huntingdon College, Windham tried to get a job as a reporter at *The Montgomery Advertiser*, but she wasn't hired because she was a woman. When all the men were drafted because of World War II, however, she finally got a job at the *Alabama Journal*. Once there she broke barriers by becoming one of the first—maybe even the first—women to cover the police beat for a major newspaper in the South. In 1944, she joined the staff of *The Birmingham News*, where she met Amasa Benjamin

Kathryn Tucker Windham has become Alabama's premier storyteller. She began her tale-telling career in the 1970s in hopes of preserving the stories of the South's people, ghosts, and places.
Courtesy of Kathryn Tucker Windham

Windham. They were married in 1946 and moved to Selma, where she became a wife and mother.

Her husband died of a heart attack in 1956, and Windham returned to reporting, joining the staff of *The Selma Times-Journal*, where she won several Associated Press awards for her writing and photography.

Windham began her second career in the 1970s, when she began traveling the South telling tales about the people, places, and things of the South. In that time, she has become Alabama's premier storyteller and a storyteller of international fame. She has written numerous books and has appeared regularly on National Public Radio's *All Things Considered*.

Her stories are those of Southern life, both of today and yesterday. Perhaps her most famous stories are those of Jeffrey, the ghost-in-residence at her home in Selma. Jeffrey first moved into Windham's Royal Street home in October of 1966 and has made regular appearances since then. It was he, she says, who inspired her to study the ghosts of Alabama. She has recorded those studies in several books and says her hope is to preserve the South's ghost stories—the true ones—before they are forgotten.

Alabamian Helen Keller was the first deaf and blind person to earn a college degree. She graduated from Radcliffe College with honors in 1904. Her home, Ivy Green, is in Tuscumbia and is open to visitors every day except holidays.

Shop 'Til You Drop

Tired of the same old stuff you find in the malls? Looking for some incredible bargains? Try shopping in Strange But True Alabama.

HARRISON BROTHERS HARDWARE • HUNTSVILLE

As Alabama's oldest operating hardware store, this establishment is an unusual combination of the practical and the historical sitting in the middle of downtown Huntsville!

Started in 1879 by brothers James and Daniel Harrison as a tobacco store on Jefferson Street, it was moved to its present location in 1897. As business progressed, the Harrison brothers (Robert and Daniel) and Robert's sons (Daniel and John) ignored modern merchandising techniques, preserving the store in its turn-of-the century condition. When John's death in 1983 spelled almost certain doom for the establishment, the

The Harrison Brothers Hardware is Alabama's oldest operating hardware store. Courtesy of Harrison Brothers Hardware

nonprofit Historic Huntsville Foundation took charge, cleaned and inventoried everything in the place, hired a manager, and reopened the doors in the fall of 1984 with a staff of dedicated volunteer clerks.

The creaky wooden floors, cozy coal stove, and hand-operated rope elevator all help to recreate an atmosphere decades old as visitors browse shelves stacked high and accessed by tall, rolling ladders. Antique biscuit jars brimming with old-fashioned candies tempt youngsters of all ages. Cotton throws, marbles by the scoop, and bird feeders are just a few of the items that will delight you whether you are looking for a special gift or are just searching for the past.

This treasure trove is located at 124 South Side Square in Huntsville.

St. Nick's Knife Factory • Orange Beach

Leave it to Alabamians to come up with this shopping combination! St. Nick's Knife Factory, formerly known as The Knife Before Christmas, is a combination knife and Christmas store.

Located at 25040 Perdido Beach Boulevard.

Unclaimed Baggage Center • Scottsboro

Wish you had back that sexy designer dress the airline lost on your last trip? Check the Unclaimed Baggage Center. It might just be there! The Unclaimed Baggage Center buys—sight unseen—luggage lost by the airlines. On any given day you can find incredible bargains on all sorts of stuff—clothes, jewelry, sports equipment, electronics—anything that can be packed and subsequently lost.

And it's not just someone's cheap skivvies, either. You might find the crème de la crème of the designer world—Rolex watches, Gucci bags, alligator shoes—and all at a fraction of the price you'd pay retail. The store claims to have more than 7,000 items for sale daily. Much of it, of course, is used (clothes are cleaned before being put up for sale), but the Unclaimed Baggage Center also buys unclaimed cargo, and these are new, in-the-box items, also offered at bargain prices.

Some real treasures have been found among the mundane items, and the owners say they never know what to expect with each new shipment. Through the years they've found such riches as a 40.95-carat natural emerald tucked away in the corner of an ordinary suitcase, a 5.8-carat wedding set hidden inside a sock, and $500 cash hidden inside a Barbie doll head.

There have been lots of oddities, too. On display in the store are a full suit of armor, and Hoggle, the ugly, life-size Jim Henson puppet used in the movie *Labyrinth*. Then there's the Egyptian artifacts dating back to BC 1500, the camera designed for the space shuttles, and the guidance system for F-16 jets—valued at a quarter of a million dollars. Those last two items were returned to the government, but what to do with that live snake found in a suitcase?

Remember how mad Mom used to get when you came home with your clothes all dirty? She'd rant about how that Alabama red clay just wouldn't come out of anything. Well, that's kinda the point with Earth Creations. This Alabama company takes perfectly clean shirts, dunks them in a soup of Alabama clay, and sells them to stores around the country. Huh. Paying good money for dirty shirts. Mom would be shocked.

Historical Events Around Alabama

From the Revolutionary War to pioneer days, from the Civil War to the Civil Rights movement, Alabamians love to take a step back in time and relive the old days.

Civil War Reenactments

Alabama has more Civil War reenactments than Carter's got liver pills (another of those unique Southern sayings). Could it be we think if we keep redoing it, one day we'll chase those damn Yankees back over the Mason-Dixon Line? Nah. It's just a good excuse to dress up in old clothes and play soldier. Here's just a mere sample of the state's yearly reenactments.

THE BATTLE FOR BRIERFIELD IRONWORKS • BRIERFIELD

With a reputation for making superior iron, this ironworks company came to the attention of Union authorities. It became a prime target for General James Wilson's campaign on

In its iron-producing heyday, Brierfield Ironworks was known as the "Magic City of Bibb County." The furnaces closed in 1894, and today, the grounds are a site for battle reenactments.
Courtesy of Brierfield Ironworks Historical State Park

Historical Events Around Alabama

Alabama's war industry sites. On March 31, 1865, the Federal 10th Missouri Cavalry, a division of Wilson's troops, attacked and burned the works within minutes.

The site was rebuilt in the 1880s and became so successful that Brierfield became known as the "Magic City of Bibb County." Unfortunately, the huge metal furnaces of Birmingham could produce ten times the amount of iron that Brierfield's brick furnaces could turn out. The furnaces closed forever in 1894.

Today, the site is a state park where battle reenactments and living history events are staged throughout the year.

Located off State Highway 25 between Montevallo and Centreville.

THE BATTLE OF DECATUR • DECATUR

It was the fall of 1864, and Union General William T. Sherman was poised to execute his blazing march through Georgia. Confederate troops, under the command of General John Hood, had spent several months battling Sherman's forces in an attempt to hold Atlanta. They had suffered many casualties and needed time to rest and regroup, but General Hood had other ideas. He believed that if he launched an attack into Tennessee that he could retake Nashville, a Yankee base of supplies, and lure Sherman out of Georgia. A quick victory there, he thought, could turn the course of the war. There was just one problem: 5,000 Yankee troops occupied Decatur, where, because of the shallow waters, he planned to cross the Tennessee River.

Hood launched an aggressive attack on Decatur, but after four grueling days of what became known as Hood's Middle Tennessee Campaign, he retreated and moved his men to Florence, forty-five miles west. High waters there forced a three-week delay in crossing, giving Yankee troops time to move into blocking positions around Nashville and put a stop to Hood's plans for a Nashville party. Instead of turning the tide of the war toward the Confederacy, Hood's campaign was a major factor in its downfall.

In addition to being a strategic location for the Confederacy, Decatur became home to Confederate General Joseph Wheeler. Known as "Fighting Joe," Wheeler was impressed with the Decatur vicinity during his many forays through the area. After the war, instead of returning to his native Georgia, he built a plantation in Courtland, west of Decatur.

Every year on Labor Day weekend, Decatur takes a step back in time and relives the days of the Civil War. In a three-day celebration called the September Skirmish, Civil War re-enactors from around the country gather for the event, which features 800 Confederate and Union troops in authentic Civil War uniforms. Staying in a living history camp, the re-enactors stage daily battles with mounted cavalry charges and marching troops. Vendors portraying camp followers, who sold provisions to the troops during the Civil War, exhibit Civil War relics and barter or sell handmade crafts.

Hosted by the Civil War reenactment groups 13th Alabama Partisan Rangers and 6th Alabama Cavalry, the event is held at Point Mallard in Decatur.

Historical Events Around Alabama

THE BATTLE OF FORT BLAKELEY • SPANISH FORT

For more than a year, the fortifications around Mobile, mainly Spanish Fort and Fort Blakeley, had discouraged a Yankee attack on the city, but in the spring of 1865, with the Confederacy crumbling, General Ulysses S. Grant decided it was time to take Mobile. A two-pronged approach was used, with troops attacking Spanish Fort from the east in the lower part of Mobile Bay and Fort Blakeley from the west out of Pensacola.

Fort Blakeley was a formidable target with forty-one artillery guns, and it was protected by several ironclads of the Confederate Navy. Those devious Yankees, led by General Fredrick Steele, moved out of Pensacola on March 20 and headed north, as if on a march to Montgomery. But fifty miles north of Pensacola, they turned south and snuck back, positioning at the rear of Fort Blakeley. On April 9, they attacked. At 16,000 to 4,000, it was hardly a fair fight, and Fort Blakeley fell within hours. Spanish Fort had fallen the day before, and with both forts captured, Mobile was easy pickin's.

The first Confederate flag was designed by a foreigner! Prussian portrait painter, Nicola Marschall, who came to Alabama in 1849, designed the Stars and Bars at the request of Mrs. Napoleon Lockett, a prominent resident of Marion. Marschall also designed one type of Confederate uniform and painted portraits of Lieutenant General Nathan Forrest and Presidents Abraham Lincoln and Jefferson Davis.

The battle at Fort Blakeley was the last major battle of the Civil War, occurring six hours after General Robert E. Lee surrendered to Grant at Appomattox. A reenactment is staged the first weekend in April at Blakeley State Park.

Located on State Highway 225 in Spanish Fort.

THE BATTLE OF MOBILE BAY • DAUPHIN ISLAND

"Damn the torpedoes! Full speed ahead!" Those words from Yankee Admiral David Farragut sealed the fate of Mobile Bay on a hot summer day in 1864. Farragut had been assigned the task of securing the Bay, and he had every intention of doing so when he entered bay waters on August 5. His fleet of eighteen Union ships received heavy fire from Forts Gaines and Morgan, but once he sailed past the forts, all that stood in his way was a small Confederate fleet—and the mines, then called "torpedoes"—that had been placed throughout the Bay. With Farragut's fateful words ringing in their ears, Union troops plowed their ships through the treacherous waters and overpowered the Confederate fleet. Before the end of the month, both Fort Gaines and Fort Morgan had fallen.

The city of Mobile, the most heavily fortified city in the Confederacy, held out until the next spring, when Union troops captured Spanish Fort and Fort Blakely, effectively ending the war. The Battle of Mobile Bay is considered one of the greatest naval battles of all time.

A reenactment of the historic clash, complete with ironclads and tall-masted ships, is staged at Dauphin Island every spring by the 6th Alabama Cavalry, a reenactment group.

Make up your mind, already! The Confederacy had three different flags and one battle flag. The battle flag was adopted after the Battle of Bull Run because there was confusion between the American flag and the Confederate Stars and Bars. The battle flag, bearing the familiar Southern Cross of stars, was adopted in September of 1861. The Confederate Navy Jack, also bearing the Southern Cross, was used by the Confederate Navy.

The second design of the official flag of the Confederacy was a field of white with the battle flag placed in the left upper corner. The field of white, however, was easily mistaken for a flag of surrender, and so, a new design was adopted in March 1865, just in time for the fall of the Confederacy the next month. This new flag added a wide red strip down the right side of the flag.

Of all the flags, the battle flag is the best known and has become a controversial symbol of the South.

THE BATTLE OF SELMA • SELMA

General Wilson was a busy man that year. After razing the Brierfield and Tannehill Ironworks, he and his men marched on, leaving a path of destruction in their wake. They reached Selma on April 1, 1865, where they battled Confederate troops led by Lieutenant General Nathan Forrest, who was famous for never losing a battle. Well, there's a first time for everything, they say, and this was it for Forrest. Outnumbered, Confederate troops were no match for the Union troops. Selma fell, and soon after, so did the Confederacy.

A reenactment of the Battle of Selma is held yearly at Battlefield Park in Selma. Activities include a grand ball—only authentic period dress allowed—and a camp dance.

LaGrange Military Academy • Muscle Shoals

Opened in 1830, Alabama's first college, LaGrange College, which later became LaGrange Military Academy, was known as the "West Point of the South." By 1862, most of the students had enlisted in the Confederate Army, and the college was closed down. The small village around it was mostly deserted. That didn't stop the Yankees. On April 28, 1863, Colonel Florence M. Cornyn and his troops, the "Destroying Angels," marched through setting fires of destruction across the valley. The college was destroyed in those fires.

A park has been established at the college site, and the pioneer village that was connected to it has been restored. Living history events, including Civil War reenactments, are held periodically throughout each year.

Located eight miles southeast of Muscle Shoals, off Highway 157.

At least part of the University of Alabama escaped LaGrange's fate. According to legend, when Union soldiers setting fire to the campus entered the front hall of the president's mansion, the president's wife, Mrs. Landon Garland, bellowed "Young man, put out that fire at once!" Being the nice young men that they were, the soldiers obediently extinguished their torches and put out the flames.

TANNEHILL IRONWORKS • MCCALLA

On the same day Brierfield Ironworks was burned, Union forces also attacked Tannehill Ironworks, just down the road in McCalla. Three companies of the 8th Iowa Cavalry raided the area and burned the ironworks to the ground.

Battle reenactments are staged at the old Tannehill Ironworks, the site of a Civil War-era blast furnace that was destroyed by the Union forces in 1865.
Courtesy of Tannehill Ironworks Historical State Park

Tannehill Ironworks is also a state park where reenactments are staged. Located off I-59, twelve miles southwest of Bessemer.

Alabama had its own Paul Revere. On a night in May 1863, Gadsden's John Wisdom jumped on his horse and rode all night to Rome, Georgia, to warn villagers that Yankee soldiers were on the way. Changing horses five times during the 67-mile ride, he yelled, "The Yankees are coming!" For that ride he earned the nickname the Paul Revere of the Confederacy.

Living History

If the Civil War isn't far enough back in time for you, don't despair! There's plenty more Alabama history to relive.

ALABAMA CONSTITUTION VILLAGE • HUNTSVILLE

Interested in how our state got started? This is the place for you! Here you can visit the actual site where forty-four delegates gathered to forge the way for Alabama statehood. Touring eight reconstructed Federal-style buildings, guests are transported back to 1819 when Alabama became the 22nd state during a Constitutional Convention. Interpreters dressed in period clothing invite visitors to participate in carding cotton,

At the Alabama Constitution Village, interpreters in period clothing invite visitors to experience Alabama's history hands-on.
Courtesy of Alabama Constitution Village

turning the great wheel lathe for the cabinetmaker, churning butter, and dipping candles.

Located at 109 Gates Avenue in Huntsville.

Alabama seceded from the Union on January 11, 1861, and for almost a month before it joined the Confederacy on February 8, was known as the Republic of Alabama. It was official, too, with a flag and everything. The flag was designed by a group of women from Montgomery. One side displayed the Goddess of Liberty holding a sword in one hand and a small flag in the other. Scrolled above her were the words "Independent Now and Forever." The flag's flip side had a cotton plant and a rattlesnake with the Latin phrase "Noli Me Tangere" (Touch Me Not). The flag flew until February 10, 1861.

THE AMERICAN VILLAGE • MONTEVALLO

The American Village is a 113-acre recreation of an eighteenth-century American town, where visitors can relive the greatest time in American history. You can debate the Declaration of Independence with Patrick Henry, sign it with Thomas Jefferson, or join George Washington's army and help rout the British.

The Revolutionary War-period village, the first of its kind in the country, was built to help educate school children on the Revolutionary War and keep alive the memory of that time.

School groups attend programs throughout the year, and casual visitors are welcome to tour at these times. Special events are staged on historical dates, such as July 4 and George Washington's birthday.

Located on State Highway 119 in Montevallo.

> In 1836, Alabama became the first state to recognize Christmas as an official holiday.

CHRISTMAS AT THE FORT • DAUPHIN ISLAND

Dauphin Island hosts a couple of living history events annually. In November there's a living history weekend that explores life on the Gulf Coast before the building of Fort Gaines. Re-enactors, dressed in pre-1840 garb, bring the past to life. You can visit settlers and families going about their daily life.

Christmas at the Fort, held in December, relives the Christmas of 1861.

The weekend is based on a letter home from Confederate soldier James M. Williams, a volunteer stationed at Fort Gaines.

THE FORT MIMS MASSACRE • BALDWIN COUNTY

By the 1800s the Upper Creek nation was angered by the continued encroachment of white settlers onto their lands. When the War of 1812 broke out, the powerful Shawnee leader Tecumseh visited the Upper Creeks and, over the protest of tribal leaders, convinced many young warriors to side with the British. They launched a series of raids against the frontier farms and settlements, initiating the Creek War, a little-known sidelight to the War of 1812. This conflict reached a crisis in August of 1814, when the Creeks, armed by the British, overpowered Fort Mims, a small outpost north of Mobile.

Despite pleas of restraint from their own leader, warriors brutally slaughtered more than 300 settlers.

Upon word of the Fort Mims massacre, Major General Andrew Jackson mustered a militia force of

On March 27, 1814, at the "horseshoe bend" in the Tallapoosa River, General Andrew Jackson's forces broke the power of the Upper Creek Indian Confederacy.
Courtesy of the National Park Service

2,000 men, supplemented with 1,000 Lower Creek and Cherokee warriors. The militia was ill trained, but after several indecisive battles, Jackson's forces attacked an Upper Creek village on a horseshoe-shaped bend in the Tallapoosa River. After allowing the women and children to cross the river to safety, Jackson and his troops wiped out the enemy force, killing more than 550 warriors. The defeat broke the Upper Creek nation, ending the Creek War and opening their rich lands to white settlers.

The battle became known as The Battle of Horseshoe Bend, and a state park has been established at the site on AL 49, near Daviston. A three-mile, round trip scenic road leads through the battleground and other associated sites. A two and eight-tenths mile history trail traverses the battlefield and a variety of natural areas. Educational activities include monthly living history demonstrations, museum exhibits, and an electronic map offering graphic details of the battle.

A reenactment of the Fort Mims Massacre is staged every year, complete with authentic dress and weapons. The event takes place at the site of Fort Mims, which has been partially restored.

Located on Fort Mims Highway in north Baldwin County.

When Big Warrior, chief of the Alabama Creeks, refused to join Tecumseh's Indian Federation, the great Shawnee chief was so angry he promised that when he returned home he would stomp his foot and cause the earth to shake, the rivers to flow backward, and the sun to disappear. Several months later, on December 16, 1811, Alabama experienced an earthquake, and indeed, the earth did shake, the Mississippi River ran backward, and a cloud of red dust obscured the sun. According to legend, the only thing left standing in Big Warrior's village was the hut in which Tecumseh stayed during his visit there.

FORT TOULOUSE/FORT JACKSON • WETUMPKA

At the invitation of the native Creeks, a group of French Colonial Marines built Fort Toulouse in 1717. Located where the junction of the Coosa and Tallapoosa rivers form the Alabama River, the fort served as a trade and military post until 1763. When the French lost the French and Indian War, they abandoned the fort, and it fell into disrepair. Only a small portion was still visible when settlers built a new earthen fort on the site in 1814, naming it Fort Jackson after General Andrew Jackson. The Treaty of Fort Jackson was signed here that year, marking the end of the Creek War.

Today, the French Fort Toulouse has been restored, and Fort Jackson has been partially restored. Monthly living history programs include both the French period and early American period. In April, a reenactment of the period of the war between the French and the British is held. In addition, Alabama Frontier Days are held annually in November. During this event, life on the frontier from 1717 until 1820 is depicted.

Located off U.S. Highway 231 in Wetumpka.

THE PIONEER MUSEUM • TROY

Just outside of Troy, the Pioneer Museum encompasses twenty-five acres containing historic log cabins, tenant houses with herb and vegetable gardens, and a one-room schoolhouse. There's also a working gristmill, a smokehouse, and a log barn. The Adams General Store is well stocked with goods from the past. More than 18,000 artifacts, including antique farm implements, dolls, and Civil War memorabilia, can be seen here. A farmer's market is held certain days of the week from May to September.

Throughout the year, the museum stages living history events where visitors can learn about pioneer life. During these events, participants dress in period costumes and perform demonstrations on pioneer life, including instruction in spinning and weaving, quilting, blacksmithing, and carpentry.

USS Alabama Battleship Memorial Park • Mobile

Drive into Mobile on Interstate 10, and you can't miss this tribute to our country's military might. It packs a whollop with vessels from sea and air to make history come alive.

OK, so the most well-known attraction here is the *USS Alabama*, winner of nine battle stars in World War II. Here you can follow in the footsteps of heroes as you tour this landmark dedicated to the memory of Alabama veterans eighteen years after she last ran under her own power. Visitors may roam the decks and see what life at sea is like, all the while viewing videos and displays of artifacts from the ship and its sailors. Better yet, stay for dinner or stay all night! Veterans are invited to dine while they reminisce at reunions held aboard ship, and overnight encampments are available for unique youth group outings.

But the Alabama isn't the only ship available for viewing—you can also see the 311-foot WW II submarine *USS Drum*, which has a permanent mooring here as well. The inside of this vessel has been painstakingly restored. Walk through it and imagine what it was like to live in such cramped quarters for days and weeks on end.

Lest we forget about aviation buffs, there are also a variety of aircraft displayed inside and outside the air-conditioned aircraft pavilion, including the A-12 Blackbird. Massive tanks, tractors, gun mounts, and gunboats used in Vietnam are also on the grounds. And if you want to do more than just look, you can get tickets for an aircraft simulator ride.

Located on Battleship Parkway in Mobile Bay.

Historical Events Around Alabama

The *USS Alabama* Battleship Museum in Mobile was used as the *USS Missouri* in 1992's *Under Siege,* starring Steven Seagal.

Free At Last

Alabama has been called the birthplace of the Civil Rights Movement. Certainly, the events that occurred here reverberate through history: Bloody Sunday—the voting rights march from Selma to Montgomery; the Sixteenth Street Church bombing; and the arrest of Rosa Parks. Their repercussions were heard throughout the country and led the way to changes in how all citizens are treated.

Reenactments are held periodically to commemorate these historic events and to honor the heroes of the Civil Rights Movement. They show us how far we've come and remind us that there's a ways to go yet.

MONTGOMERY

It was December 1, 1955, and Rosa Parks, an African-American, had just finished a long day at work as a seamstress at a Montgomery department store. Boarding the bus for home, she bypassed the front Whites Only section and settled into a seat in the middle of the bus, where African-Americans were allowed to sit if the bus was not full.

In 1955, Montgomery seamstress, Rosa Parks, was arrested for refusing to give up her bus seat to white passengers. Because of the ensuing bus boycott, the Supreme Court declared Montgomery's segregation laws unconstitutional on November 13, 1956.
Associated Press

Free At Last

After several stops the front of the bus filled, and the bus driver ordered all African-Americans to move to the back of the bus. No one moved at first, but upon his second order, all the African-Americans seated in the middle section moved to the back of the bus, except Rosa Parks. She was tired. Tired from a long day at work. Tired of the treatment she received in restaurants. Tired of being asked to move to the back of the bus. Tired of being treated like a second-class citizen. Today, she wasn't moving.

Furious, the bus driver pulled the emergency brake, marched back to where Parks was sitting, and again demanded that she move to the back of the bus. Again, she refused. The driver left the bus and returned with a police officer, who promptly arrested Parks for violating segregation laws.

Parks's bravery that day marked a turning point in the fight against segregation. Fed up with the treatment of African-Americans in Montgomery, local civil rights leaders, including new minister Dr. Martin Luther King Jr., vowed to fight bus segregation. They appealed Parks's arrest to the Supreme Court and called for a bus boycott, an action that was sure to hurt the bus line, since 75 percent of its riders were African-Americans. In a phenomenal show of unity, the city's 17,000 African-American residents found other modes of transportation and implemented the boycott despite violent repercussions. It took almost a year, but finally on November 13, 1956, the Supreme Court declared Montgomery's segregation laws unconstitutional.

The next time you wonder what one person can do, think of Rosa Parks. And remember that she is an Alabamian.

The Rosa Parks Library and Museum serves as a reminder of this milestone event in the struggle for civil rights and equality for all individuals. Interpretive exhibits and artifacts tell the story of a courageous act that changed America and redirected the course of history. The library and museum are located on Montgomery Street in Montgomery.

SELMA

The name of this town is synonymous with this country's civil rights struggle. Events that took place here brought national attention to the state and helped to bring about the Voting Rights Act of 1965. On March 7, 1965—"Bloody Sunday"—600 civil rights marchers began a march out of Selma on U.S. Route 80. Just six blocks away, on the Edmund Pettus Bridge, state and local police attacked the marchers with billy clubs and tear gas, driving them back into Selma. Two days later, Martin Luther King Jr. led a symbolic march to the bridge.

For the third march, civil rights leaders sought and received court protection, and on March 21, 1965, 3,200 marchers set out for Montgomery. They walked twelve miles a day and slept in fields along the way. By the time they reached the state capitol on March 25, their numbers had swelled to 25,000. Less than five months later, President Lyndon Johnson signed the Voting Rights Act of 1965.

The bridge remains a monument to courageous people who took part in this history-making event.